Your Guide to Self-actualization

Your Guide to Self-actualization

How To Be Happy, Successful, And Free

Make the rest...the best

Gay Patricia Matheson

To order additional copies of this book, contact: Xlibris
844-714-8691
www.Xlibris.com
Orders@Xlibris.com
830583

Dedication

To Dean, the love of my life, a dream come true I didn't even know I was dreaming.

And to all my incredible clients who had the courage to roll up their sleeves and do the work necessary to transform their lives.

Contents

Contents

Introduction

If you haven't seen the classic film *The Wizard of Oz* with Judy Garland, I highly suggest you get it and watch it. If you've already seen it, I urge you to watch it again. There couldn't be a more perfect metaphor for reaching your full potential or becoming *self-actualized*.

In the beginning, we find the main character, Dorothy, living in a black-and-white world (dissatisfaction). Consumed by fear of loss, she finds herself lost and afraid. In spite of this, Dorothy's drive to get home (becoming self-actualized) pushes her to begin her search. In doing so, the Good Witch (her spiritual guide) magically appears to help her. With the support and direction of the Good Witch, Dorothy begins her journey. And as she does, her world transforms into brilliant color.

. I think there is some part in all of us that yearns for something more, that place, "somewhere over the rainbow," where we're happy, successful, and free. Call it the soul's song, the deep part of ourselves long forgotten and obscured by our busy daily lives. When a baby pops out of the womb, what you see is authentic. The baby may be laughing one moment, crying the next, and then laughing once again. It moves fluidly through all its emotions with ease. Not a trace of inhibition. *They are alive with feelings!* Their life at this point is like a color television. They haven't learned to suppress their feelings or to make a good presentation. These things happen over time. Gradually, we learn to adapt to our circumstances so as not to be abandoned or to experience pain. We unconsciously ingest familial and societal programs and develop a vast array of coping mechanisms. When we suppress our feelings, we suppress *all our feelings*. It's not as if we can suppress the pain without muting the pleasure as well. It's a dulling out of our aliveness, which is the full experience of all our feelings. Slowly but surely, we move from a life of aliveness and color to a new baseline of black and white. The world of black and white that develops over time is more of a flatline. We still have high times, like getting a promotion, or low times, the family dog dies, but basically, we have sacrificed our *aliveness* in life for perceived safety.

The goal of this book is to show you how to live in brilliant color once again. To experience the aliveness of life joyously, with all its ups and downs. You see, that "somewhere over the rainbow" isn't a place, it's a state of mind, and it's available to all of us. And I'm going to show you how to get it, and in the process, you will realize how amazing you are and how juicy it is to live life happy, successful, and free.

Chapter 1

Magic

So what is self-actualization anyway? The German psychiatrist, Kurt Goldstein, coined the word, but it was the psychologist, Abraham Maslow, in the last century, who made it famous. Abraham Maslow came along and studied the healthiest of people; he wanted to know the qualities and characteristics that made them so. He considered self-actualization the highest level of psychological development an individual could attain, and it's composed of the top 1% of society. Self-actualization contends that individuals are motivated to fulfill their potential, a desire that could lead to realizing one's capabilities. Self-actualization is growth-motivated rather than deficiency-motivated. In other words, self-actualization does not stem from a lack of something but from a desire to be more, to be larger than we thought we were.

What makes a person self-actualized? Simple, *they have created the life they want.* They are doing what they want to provide for themselves; they find joy and passion in their careers. They make the kind of income they want; that might be $40,000 a year as a gardener or $500,000 a year as a CEO of a company. The amount doesn't matter; the point is they make what they want to make. They have the love interests they want to have. This could be a traditional love relationship, or it could be a seventy-year-old woman with a circle of great friends, or it could be someone running an ashram, an orphanage, or a pet rescue. Once again, these individuals are able to produce what they want, and what do they get from it? Satisfaction and joy. That doesn't mean their situations remain static. If new needs, desires or situations arise, self-actualized individuals are able to adapt, pivet, and once again create a fulfilling life for themselves.

In the movie *The Wizard of Oz*, we find Dorothy dissatisfied with life, living in a world of black and white. Along comes a tornado that uproots everything in Dorothy's world. It's like what happens in our lives when we realize life is not enough without passion, excitement, and joy. From there, Dorothy begins her journey, and *she steps into color.* Though her journey is hard, *it's brilliantly alive with color.* And in the end, it was navigating all the obstacles that got her to where she wanted to be—*home.*

Happiness *is* our home; it's where we are meant to be. I believe it's our birthright. I can't imagine that we exist on the earth without the capacity to make our lives great and achieve happiness. That's what drove me to therapy at forty. I had been to therapy for situational problems over the years, but I never committed to real self-analysis. My life was not bad, it just felt as if something was missing. Something was eluding me, and I couldn't put my finger on it. I had high times and low times, successes and failures, just like everyone else, but there was an undercurrent of unease that I was only vaguely aware of. I wondered what it would be like to be completely contented and joyous in life, that sounded like enlightenment to me. But I didn't know how to get there. Throughout the years, I tried many different things: read a million books; attended workshops, seminars, and retreats; implemented various programs, strategies, and systems. You name it, I tried it. I am grateful for all these things as each of these brought me yet to another level of awareness. But far and away, it was through the examining of my own mind through therapy that started turning my life into an exciting adventure that I continue to enjoy today. This is what inspired me to be a therapist: I wanted to help others achieve the same juicy life that I was able to achieve and maintain. That's why I wanted to write this book—to help others learn to unlock the door of their own happiness.

Happiness is a code. Once you know the code, the doors swing wide. Magic and happiness come rushing in. Without the code, you could try the million or more combinations throughout eternity and nothing would happen. It's like a vault; with the combination, it's easy; without it, it's hopeless. Remember Dorothy; she endured a long arduous journey, fraught with dangers and obstacles, only to find at the very end that all she had to do was click her heels together three times and she would be home.

Making life great and being happy does not have to be dramatic; we don't have to be a star or make millions of dollars. In fact, if you look at Hollywood, you can see that this is exactly *not* the case. To have a sense of expression, love, and contentment in our lives, that's living a life embodying happiness. Freud said, "To love and to work successfully, that is a successful life."

This is a magical book. Because if you can break free of your self-imposed limitations; *yours can be a magical life*. So what is magic really? What looks like magic to the observer is really skill, strategy, and technique to the magician. This is an awesome realization because anyone can acquire skills, learn strategies and techniques. You hear people say, "Oh, he's just lucky," or "She was born with a natural talent." Even though luck and natural talent are real occurrences, they don't ensure a successful life will follow. Think of all the lottery winners who end up broke three to five years after winning. Everybody knows someone who is chock-full of potential who ends up doing nothing. I had a friend who was crazy smart and creative to boot, but he didn't want to work. Instead of finding work that he loved and that would feed him, financially and otherwise, he spent his time devising ways to get out of work and tried every scheme to get rich quick. Unfortunately, life went by, and disappointment led to bitterness. Disappointment is a part of life, but resilience is the characteristic that frees us from its grasp.

Imagination is the yellow brick road that can lead you to happiness. Like the Scarecrow, the Tin Man, and the Cowardly Lion, all you need is a brain, a heart, and courage. You are not reliant on anyone else or anything else to make this happen. If you take full responsibility for yourself, you might just attract a guide. In fact, you've already attracted me by picking up this book. Let me introduce myself, call me the Good Witch. I'm willing and committed to being your guide, provided *you* are committed to rolling up your sleeves and doing whatever is necessary to achieve happiness in your life. If you go through these pages, and honestly assess yourself, you will be able to create a roadmap of a new territory, a territory of passion, excitement, and contentment. Don't take my word for it; find out for yourself.

When I ask myself what excites me the most in life, it's helping people transform their lives into amazing lives where they are fully and joyfully engaged. This book includes a variety of elements that go into uncovering a healthy Self, the prerequisite to achieving happiness. I say uncovering because, just like Dorothy in *The Wizard of Oz*, the healthy Self was always there. Years of cultural and familial programming have obscured its essence. Once we rediscover our healthy Self, we now have a structure that's capable of creating and supporting great things. Remember, without a solid foundation, buildings will crumble. You may already be looking at your life and seeing evidence of those "crumblings": It could be with your career. It could be in your relationships. It could be with your kids, your parents, your neighbors, your finances, or your retirement. "Is that all there is?" is not an uncommon refrain. Don't let that discourage you. The healthy, happy essence is there; it just needs to be uncovered.

I've included many personal and client stories (names, genders, and situations have been changed) that exemplify the transcendence process and help you identify elements and solutions. You will see how we each create our own heaven and hell on earth by our thoughts, beliefs, and behaviors.

Read each chapter, and honestly evaluate where you are with each characteristic. If an important characteristic is weak, zero in and beef it up with the recommended methods. If it's strong, enjoy your success in that area and move on. The questions and comments at the end of each chapter will help you assess where you are and where you need work. Remember, nothing is impossible with will, commitment, and determination. *My wish for you is that you will create and enjoy the life you truly want. By the end of this book, I promise you, you will be on the road to self-actualization. And with each chapter along the way, you will experience expanded happiness, success, and freedom.*

Are you willing to do whatever it takes to get the life you want and to experience a magical life of happiness, success, and freedom? If so, follow me.

Chapter 2

Possibility

After more than two decades of practicing psychotherapy and working with hundreds of clients, I have come to realize that many people enter their middle years totally unprepared, even if they think they're prepared. I hear things like, "I never imagined it would turn out this way," or "I'm living out my plan, but it's not doing it for me. "I'm unsatisfied in my relationship, but heck, I'm in my sixties." Is that all there is?" or "I'm so disappointed with my kids, my spouse, my parents, my career, my friends." You name it. Then there are the younger ones in their thirties, forties, and fifties who fear getting older; they are afraid to lose their looks, their virility, their children, their careers. All may have meticulously planned their financial future so as to not outlive their money. But they have failed to consider their psychological future, wherein one can find happiness and contentment with a well-thought-out, albeit flexible, strategy.

Eric Erickson was the psychologist who came along in the last century and defined the stages of development we go through in life. He coined the last stage of life as "integrity versus despair." If we've lived life fully and are satisfied, then we experience integrity. If we look back at our lives and we're filled with regret and disappointment, we experience despair. I call the last stage in life the fourth quarter, not only because it really is the fourth quarter of our life, but also because we have the ability to pull a great win out of the game in the fourth. If we feel like we played it well, the result is integrity: feeling good about how we lived our life. But we don't have to wait until the fourth quarter to scramble to put a good life together.

About 2,500 years ago, it was Socrates who said, "The unexamined life is not worth living." Why? Because if you don't examine your life on a regular basis, how can you make it better? This starts with taking control of your mind. The mind is like a wild stallion that will drag you around like a ragdoll if you let it. The idea is to direct that stallion. With your direction (focused intention) and that powerhouse beneath you (your amazing mind), anything is possible. Our minds are mighty minds. If you roll up your sleeves and explore how *your* mind works, how it defends against unwanted emotions and incorporates coping mechanisms that no longer serve you, you can transform your world, guaranteed. And the quality of your life is totally and completely your responsibility and yours alone.

In the midst of my excitement about the prospect of helping a wider audience find a better way to roll with and enjoy the complexities of life today, along came the coronavirus. That changed everything. Everything became immediate and uncertain. It occurred to me that what was needed to deal with the coronavirus, and the ensuing economic downturn, was the same thing that was needed to have a fabulous life: intelligence and resilience. We'll talk about those more in the upcoming chapters.

This book contains powerful elements and characteristics that, if embraced, will make for an outstanding life. Yes, you can jettison yourself into the top 1 percent, the self-actualized, with a little character development. I wish I had had the knowledge and skill in my early years, but that's in the rearview mirror now. And hey, wisdom has to be earned. Each year I gained more knowledge and skill, making life more enjoyable every step of the way. Here's the key: When you get the knowledge, *you must apply it. And it's never too late.* I'm reminded of a film clip I saw of Chuck Berry and Keith Richards of the Stones. They were playing a song that Chuck Berry wrote, and Chuck Berry stopped cold, frustrated with the way Keith Richards was playing. He turned to Keith and snapped, "It's like *this*," and he showed him.

Keith Richards replied, "Yeah, yeah, I know, I know . . ."

Then Chuck Berry barked at Richards, "Then realize it!"

We can *know* something, but *realizing* it is a different matter. Think of that, realizing, *making something real, operational in your life.*

Look at each characteristic with ruthless honesty. Then give yourself a rating of 1–5, 1 being that characteristic is great, you've got that handled, and 5 means that characteristic is a disaster and needs a lot of work. This makes it easy. If you want to build up your quads, you go to a trainer or buy a book that can give you the knowledge you need. Then you apply the knowledge. The beauty is, as you develop each characteristic, you begin to feel happier and happier, then the good feelings become the motivation to stay on track and continue.

Think of life as a wonderful dance; you've learned different dance steps all along the way, and you will definitely want to learn some new moves, but now you're going to pull it all together for a golden epic era. Be determined to make the rest the best. And remember, you're not alone on this journey. I'll be with you every step of the way.

My friend, Mary Pat, a landscape designer, describes it best. She says life is like a beautiful garden: You've got to design it. You've got to weed, trim, and clear out all the dead parts ongoingly. And you've got to keep it fed and watered. In other words, your life is your garden to design and tend. Most of all, you want to feel joyful in it.

What are some possibilities for you if you aren't limiting yourself? Choose two or three possibilities that excite you.

Chapter 3

Resilience

Resilience is an amazing quality; it is the ability to bounce back *no matter what*, to be elastic and flexible to rise and meet any occasion.

Resilience is the basis of self-esteem and confidence and the forerunner of success in every area. The good news about resilience is that it can be cultivated, and that's where intelligence comes in. And to add more good news, the new neural science tells us that intelligence can be developed and expanded at any age.

The years just keep on rolling by. We couldn't wait to be adults: to fall in love; to start a career; to have a family; to buy our first house, a great car, perhaps a second home in the mountains or by the beach. Now we've done all those things, and our kids are launched (hopefully, lol). So how do we create a rich, full life with meaning *today*?

When I lived in Seattle in the '70s, I remember hearing about a study of Boeing executives. For the most part, in that time, people generally had one job until retirement; that could be thirty to forty years. Turns out, the executives at Boeing lived an average of only six months after retirement. *What?* Well, if you think about it, their whole adult lives, they identified with being an executive at Boeing. When they retired, who were they? Many were lost and did not have the wherewithal to reinvent themselves and to reinvent their lives. Or to put more accurately, they didn't understand the *necessity* of doing so. Or how about the mother who builds her whole life around her children? Who is she when the mother role is over? What happens when a couple who have been married for forty years decides to divorce, or when a long-term partner dies? All those years identifying with being a couple, what now? Sometimes friends of the couple can't even make the transition. Did you ever hear of someone becoming single again for whatever reason, and their friends that are couples disappear? Adapting is dealing with "what is" and then doing our best to work with it. We were born to create, and resilience is the ability to recreate ourselves based on the new circumstances we find ourselves in. Nietzsche said, "Philosophy is just another stage in life." In other words, different contexts require different responses.

What about the person who spent the first twenty years of their life growing with a company that then was let go as a result of downsizing? I'm reminded of the old VCR stores that sprung up overnight and were everywhere. Then along came Netflix, Amazon Prime, etc. In a flash, the video stores disappeared. The world is constantly changing, and we need to be elastic and flexible to meet the challenges that come our way. And challenges *always* come our way. When we are "fixed," our energy contracts. In martial arts, we're taught, when we are fixed, someone can topple us easily. When we are flexible, we can easily redirect the energy coming toward us back to our opponent. An old metaphor depicts this: "If the branch is flexible, it moves with the wind. If it is rigid, it will snap." Being flexible is expansive; it allows us to entertain all the possibilities.

When I think of resilience, I think of the Navy SEALs. Some people think they are one-dimensional brute-force men. But they're not; nothing could be further than the truth. They are multifaceted. They are trained in many things beyond the physical. Their minds are trained—big time— by their internal will to master themselves. Experts, they have a code of excellence; they are scholars in many ways. Why is this important? Because they never know what the mission will require. You can plan a mission and rehearse it a thousand times (and they do), but you can never foresee all the variables that might arise on execution. Just one of those variables has the ability to tear the mission plan to shreds. Then something different may be required. The SEALs code is to never give up, and if one door closes, they make sure another one opens. Their success comes from flexibility, adapting to whatever circumstances they're presented with. Remember what Charles Darwin said, "It's not the strongest of the species that survive, nor the most intelligent, but the one most responsive to change." Hence, the Seals success rate is off the charts.

How you adapt to change is largely how you interpret events to yourself. This is a true story from a Green Beret captain. His sergeant led a six-man crew behind enemy lines, and this is what the sergeant radioed back, "The Viet Cong have us surrounded Captain, they won't get away now!"

Another military man shared that their team was dropped at a particular location and their weapons were also to be dropped, but somehow this did not happen. The captain saw an enemy encampment over the hill and yelled, "There are all the weapons we need, let's go get them!"

Resilience was the only thing that kept my husband Dean and I from crumpling to the floor in despair in 1999. We interned at a clinic where we were supervised. As an intern, you cannot practice psychotherapy without a supervisor. We worked hard to establish our practices, we wrote articles and gave talks in the community, we saw thirty clients a week at a discounted rate, and now we were ready to take the test for licensure. We had completed our three thousand hours, our practices were thriving, and we were making good money for ourselves and the clinic. In the process of buying a house, we were optimistic; all those years of hard work had paid off. Then just weeks before we were scheduled to take our final exam, the unimaginable happened: We were fired with no warning.

The owner of the clinic thought it was an opportunity to steal our clients as we couldn't practice without a supervisor, and we weren't yet licensed. With the prospect of losing our incomes and being in the process of buying a house, we walked out of the clinic in shock. We had to work fast. We delayed the test as we were in no emotional condition to take it. Then I set out to secure an office, while Dean headed out to hire a supervisor for us. We called all our clients and explained the situation honestly to them. We told them they could continue to see us, but they couldn't call us their therapists; they would have to call us life coaches. All our clients came with us. In four weeks, we were up and running, furnishing our office with furniture from consignment stores and making our full fee rather than the 60/40 split we had at the clinic. What looked like something horrendous turned out to be of great benefit. Not only were we able to put together an office in record time, enjoy 100 percent of our income, but we also became the first licensed life coaches in the Palm Springs area.

I worked with a woman once who had lost her husband of almost sixty years; he was her best friend, and they did everything together. Rose changed nothing in her house; all his clothes were still in the closet. Her children urged her to come and see me as she had been crying every day since his death three years before. Her friends tried to convince her to play bridge with them or to go golfing, but to no avail. She berated herself and wondered what was wrong with her that she wouldn't take her friends up on their kind offers. When asked if she enjoyed golf and bridge, Rose said that she didn't, she never had. I told her that there was nothing wrong with her. If she didn't like those activities before, why would she like them now?

Rose's children were scheduled to come over and go through her husband's things and get rid of them because she said she couldn't bear to do it. I suggested that she call her kids and cancel so she could go through his things on her own. I told her it's okay to cry as long and as hard as she wanted to until she emptied. Going through his clothes and getting rid of them was *accepting the reality that he was gone*. She took eighteen big garbage bags of his clothes to Goodwill. Then we started to look at who Rose was currently and who she wanted to be. Rose had a Master's Degree in Psychology and loved learning, so we explored lectures and classes that were available in the desert as well as through the senior centers. She had always wanted to write, so she found a writers group in the area. She made new friends through her new activities and was able to find the joy in life once again. Rose came by the office just to tell me she hadn't cried for months.

Think of the resilience of vets that come home with limbs missing, and then they make it their mission to help other vets or other people with disabilities. Or how about a young woman who was raped and barely escaped being murdered who then decided to teach self-defense classes to women? These are heroes who inspire us because they have *courage*; they turned lemons into lemonade. They refused to give up, and they somehow created new meaning in their lives. There's a beautiful Taoist saying: "The obstacle in the way *is* the way."

In other words, tough times show us exactly what we need to learn. We can develop resiliency by first noticing how we react to the challenges that come our way. Then we can identify with the warrior and *choose* how we want to respond. The warrior responds with courage and determination. Conscious choice is the difference between being a victim or the victor. Remember, every time we hit an obstacle or disappointment with resilience, we're expanding our esteem and confidence, which, in turn, makes us feel good.

Take some time and notice how you've reacted to the challenges that have come your way in the last five years. How could you have reacted differently to get better results?

Close your eyes and identify with being a victim. How does it feel? Now close your eyes and identify with being a warrior. How does it feel? Notice the difference.

Chapter 4

Intelligence

There's a big difference between IQ and intelligence from my perspective. Someone can have an IQ that's off the charts, but that doesn't mean they're going to make intelligent decisions and choices. Intelligence is the ability to acquire *and apply* knowledge and skills; in other words, to learn what works and what doesn't work, along with the ability and *will* to apply it. Intelligence is not passive; *it's active*. We're born with an IQ, but the sky's the limit in terms of intelligence.

I've worked with many very smart individuals whose lives were not working or parts of their lives were not working. And by the way, there's no shame in that; it happens to all of us. The shame is in not figuring it out. Not unlike J. Paul Getty, who said, "I'd give all my millions for one successful marriage." Really? You were the richest man in the world at one time, and you couldn't figure out how to have a successful relationship? You couldn't go to a therapist, a life coach, or a pastor to explore your relationship dynamics? This is where *will* comes in. You've heard that old expression: "Where there's a will, there's a way." Actually, will is the power that *creates* a way. And will is something that can be developed.

Sometimes our life is great, except for this one little thing that continues to be a thorn in our side. Sometimes our life is just good, and we yearn for great, but we fear that's unrealistic or that it couldn't happen to us. Don't believe it! Life can be great if we are determined to make it so. Intelligence is having the courage and fortitude to examine all the parts to see what's working and what isn't. Why can't you just live life without examining it? Well, you can, if you want life to remain the same. Many people do just that. Great individuals in business understand this concept intuitively. If you're not constantly evaluating what's working and what isn't working in your business, you'll soon be circling the drain. And different periods or economic conditions require different solutions. You could be on the crest of some new development and need to go all out. Or you could be at the beginning of a downturn and need to scale down. The point is, in business or in life, you need to be aware of what's happening and have the flexibility to adjust.

Intelligence also helps us determine what to value. Tina was a teacher, and she was hot for a brand-new top-of-the-line BMW. Given her income, I knew the payment would restrict her lifestyle and quickly become a burden. When asked why the BMW was so important to her, I heard all the usual answers: "I love a car that performs well and makes me feel like I'm really in charge of the road. It has tons of features: I love the feel of the leather, it has incredible speed, which makes me feel safe, *and it's really sexy." Now we're getting somewhere.*

With continued questioning, Tina finally admitted she thought she'd look fabulous in the car with the top down. I could see the glamour shot of herself in her mind. When I pointed out to her that she was putting more value in an image than actually providing a good life for herself, unencumbered by hefty debt, she was able to make a more intelligent choice.

In my earlier life, I was a stockbroker. When I first arrived on the scene, Bill, a fellow stockbroker, was gracious enough to carry my things into the office for me. Eighty years old, a stockbroker for over fifty years, Bill was a fabulous individual, and we became fast friends. I learned a lot from Bill. Most of the brokers in the office were men, and they would constantly rib Bill to his face and behind his back about the car he drove, among other things. His car was twenty years old. Now Bill had a paid-for house, with five bedrooms and five bathrooms, right on the beach in Santa Barbara. He put his six kids through college, and when his wife's brother and wife were killed in a car accident, Bill raised those six children and put them through college. He could have bought and sold the other arrogant brokers a hundred times over. When I asked him if the ribbing bothered him, this is what he said, "I know who I am. I don't need to impress anyone."

Intelligence is knowing when to act and knowing when not to act. In martial arts, the goal is to avoid a fight. But if a fight presents itself, then the goal is to win that fight. Roth, was a client who built a very successful business that began to take on a life of its own. It had provided him with a wonderful living, but he was now mid-fifties and completely burned out. The business had a lot of moving parts that constantly had to be monitored and fine-tuned. Roth tried many different strategies with the business to reduce his stress, but in the end, the business just kept growing, and his stress grew with it. He told me he hated his life. What good is a ton of money if you hate your life? Roth was willing to take the scary risk of letting his business go, and lo and behold, other wonderful opportunities presented themselves. And by the way, he makes more money now than he ever did in his business. Funny how when you let go of something you don't enjoy, the released energy produces far-better outcomes.

I remember in the beginning of my relationship with my husband, Dean, we got in a huge fight in the car when I shared some feelings. I was going to therapy at the time, and I told my therapist about it. He said, "Why would you bring that up in the car? The car isn't a place to bring up your feelings. That should be done at home, without distractions, to give them the import they deserve."

Six months later, I was upset about something, we were in the car, and I wanted to get it off my chest. My therapist's words danced across my brain, but I overrode them and launched anyway. The result? Same as the last time, an explosion. I hadn't yet learned how to tolerate my anxiety so as to appropriately time things to get the best result. Did I mention that I was a slow learner?

When I was a teenager and my dad would get home from work, I'd start "working him" for something I wanted. One day my mother took me aside and said, "If you'd just let your dad change his clothes and relax for a little while, he'd probably be far more receptive to any request you might have." I experimented, and it worked like magic, knowing when to act and when not to act—*timing*. That's intelligence.

Intelligence is knowing your weak areas and being on guard for them. And more than being on guard, taking active steps to beef up the weak areas. I have had many clients who have had major anger problems. They created huge dramas and upsets in their lives with terrible ramifications.

Some of them have actually driven a loving partner out of their life because the partner had had enough. This is generally unresolved childhood issues, feelings that have been repressed for years. Sometimes this repressed material comes out in other ways, like fibromyalgia or debilitating back pain. People don't want to explore these feelings because it's painful. But is it more painful than being contrite after causing a huge blow-out, losing the one you love, a job, or experiencing chronic pain? Many of my clients operate in the opposite way; they repress their feelings, and they don't support themselves by having a voice. Clients of all kinds have weak boundaries that cause major problems in their lives. All our weak areas can be strengthened; we just need to be *aware*. When we notice we're getting negative results, we can easily identify the weak area and get to work.

Intelligence is knowing when to keep going and when to quit. I once worked with a female surgeon who proudly announced that she had completed every single thing that she ever started. To give you an idea, Susan became a champion marathon runner while completing her residency! By the time I saw her, she had experienced a mental breakdown and was completely worn out and disenchanted with life. I asked her if she would stay in a relationship in which there was physical abuse. "Of course not!" How about finishing a terrible meal in a restaurant? I explained that while her philosophy of completing everything she started was admirable in many ways, it also confined her to a life of drudgery, if she didn't allow herself the freedom to choose. Rigidity can make us *feel* safe but doesn't actually *make* us safe.

David and Diane had many years of marriage behind them but were constantly at each other's throats. They communicated by criticizing each other. Sex was a thing of the past. The reality was they met when they were young and life was just an ongoing party. As they got older, David started focusing on his health. He quit drinking, started exercising and eating in a healthy way. Diane was more involved with her business and partying after hours with all her business associates. In this case, with two divergent lifestyles and philosophies, there was no way a deeply-satisfying relationship could be maintained. They were mad at each other because the "other" no longer shared a common perspective on life. They each kept trying to get their partner to come around to their point of view. Neither person was wrong or bad; they just had vastly different views on how they wanted to live their lives. It was futile, of course, and they decided to end the marriage. David revealed to me how hard it was to end the relationship. I replied, "Yes, it is but not nearly as hard as continuously trying to force a square peg into a round hole."

They now have the opportunity to be happy, to find partners who share their values and their perspectives on life.

Sarah's mother told her she was a quitter when she was young. When she was in her third year of college, she realized she did not like her major, but she pushed through because she didn't want to be viewed as a "quitter." A few years later, she had to come to grips with the fact that she did not enjoy her field and now had to re-educate herself in another area. She could have done that in her junior year, saving herself a lot of time and strife, but she did not want to be labeled a "quitter." In reality, she was never a quitter. Did she quit some things? Yes, but always appropriately, after they had outlived their usefulness, like leaving ballet behind after fifteen years. Never underestimate how our early formative years play a part in our lives. We need to be aware so that our old programming is not running our lives today.

Sometimes we want to stop doing something just because it's hard. Intelligence will keep us on track until we achieve the desired goal. A perfect example is couples when they come to therapy. They're having trouble, and therefore, they need to establish new ways of communicating, learn new skills, and come up with new solutions. Okay, but they've been doing things the same way for their whole life, they don't wanna. Resistance is a fierce force. Change is hard, but staying in misery is harder if you think about it. When Dean and I first went to couples therapy many years ago, we almost scared one therapist out of her office. Then we found a therapist who really knew what she was doing. It was *hard work*; we had to learn a new way of communicating (different from what we got from our families), master ourselves and our emotions, and put new skills and strategies in place. I kid you not, it was exhausting. By the time we got to therapy, I don't think either one of us cared if the relationship made it or not. But to quit would have been a colossal mistake. We now have a ten relationship that is beyond our wildest dreams and provides us with innumerable and continuous pleasures. It was hard work but totally worth it.

Looking at intelligence as a verb, it's the key to success in this journey to happiness and freedom. It's the ability to take in new knowledge *and apply it*. Remember, every choice and decision has meaning and consequence, so choose wisely. And every wise choice takes you closer to that wonderful life that's filled with happiness and satisfaction.

Without judgment, think of some of the choices you've made in the past. Follow them through to the end. Then evaluate whether you were acting with intelligent awareness or driven by an emotional component.

Think of some of the choices that are in front of you now. How can you intelligently assess to get the best possible outcome for yourself?

Chapter 5

Reframing

Life is a cosmic play of epic proportions. It helps to see it as a comedy, but really, it also incorporates all the elements of a Shakespearean tragedy. Most of our problems are man-made or, more accurately, *mind-made*. What does that mean?

It means our perceptions and reactions are entirely on us. We are totally responsible for them. The brilliant part is if we take complete responsibility for our perceptions and reactions, we then have the power to change them. And that, my friends, is a friggin' miracle in the making. You grab hold of that, and you've got the world by the tail. Our incredible mind creates our heaven or hell, and most of us are oblivious to the enormous power we have. Remember Shakespeare, "There is nothing either good or bad, that thinking makes it so."

"Reframing" is perhaps one of the most effective ways to change your attitude about a situation quickly. Reframing is the ability to interpret or frame things in such a way so as to diminish uncomfortable and/or painful feelings and enhance positive feelings. Since happiness is based a great deal on contentment, the ability to shift (reframe) your perspective from half empty to half full is a skill worth mastering. Most people think happiness is found in external events. The problem with this limited view is it keeps us victims of our circumstances. If we believe happiness lies mostly in our state of mind, now we have the ability to shape our own perspectives. We can be flexible and creative in our outlook and, therefore, our solutions. Anyone can get good at reframing, you just have to learn how. I call this creative flexibility of perception. It's fun to practice because as you challenge yourself to change a negative perception into a positive perception, you'll find that your feelings will follow. Thus, you are *choosing* to turn negative feelings into positive feelings. Who in their right mind wouldn't want to do that?

Awareness is the ticket to creating the reality we want.

Let's say you get a new job that entails commuting for an hour. You can complain endlessly about what a drag it is and destroy your satisfaction and excitement about getting a new job, or you can look on the bright side and tell yourself, "Great, now I have time to listen to those audio books I haven't had time for."

Or you could think to yourself how glad you are to have some quiet time every day to collect your thoughts. The first way of thinking creates a bummer; the second, good feelings. Which would you rather have, heaven or hell? Realize that with every interpretation you are choosing.

Maybe you find your favorite condo in Hawaii is booked during your time off this year, and you were really looking forward to spending your vacation there. Once again, you can be completely upset and ruin your day, or you can use this opportunity to investigate new places that you might like even better. Maybe you're disappointed that your adult kids won't be joining you on a group vacation this year. Perhaps this would be a good opportunity to reconnect with your spouse in a different way.

One day, in the 120-degree heat of summer, I was complaining to myself about the heat, and I brought to mind all the gray, rainy, damp, dreary days in Seattle, where I grew up. Instantly, my perspective changed (I did choose to live in the desert after all), and I was filled with appreciation for the ever-blue sky of the desert. First, I was bummed, then I was delighted.

One of the best examples of reframing happened with a client many years ago. Tom came to me struggling with depression. This well-dressed business man expressed that he felt like a complete failure, an utter loser. I asked him how it was that he came to this opinion of himself. He said he didn't make enough money. "How much money do you make?" I asked him.

He said, "$250,000."

Now at that time, $250,000 was probably in the top 1 percent of the country, not to mention the world, and I told my client that. Tom had three homes and five cars. I shared with him some of the statistics of the time. "Do you realize only 4 percent of the world has a car and sometimes just one car that many people share? More often than not, many people share a house or an apartment, sometimes many generations share a small dwelling. So . . . is it really accurate to put yourself in the loser category when, in reality, you are in the top 1 percent?"

He couldn't deny the facts. As I was reviewing the statistics with him, I could see his energy starting to shift. He started feeling better about himself, then pretty good about himself. Same guy, same life, nothing had changed in his circumstances. He walks in depressed, walks out feeling good. What happened? Tom simply changed his perception, and that can happen with a snap of your fingers. *That's* the amazing power of your mind.

Why did Tom distort reality in that negative way to begin with? Turns out, Tom had created a very successful business providing high-ticket items to wealthy clients, most of whom were old money. As a result of his business, he was always rubbing shoulders with his wealthy clients. At first, he was thrilled to have this thriving business with clients who could easily afford the goods he sold. But over time he began to compare himself to them and found that he continuously came up short. It's hard to compete with old money. In fact, comparing, in general, is the kiss of death; there will always be people who are smarter, more talented, richer, more beautiful or handsome, you get the picture. If you want to be happy, it's best to drop comparing out of your repertoire. This is where your mind comes in, make a different choice. You can choose what you think about. Your feelings will follow. My client made the change, I had nothing to do with it. I simply presented a different perspective, and Tom was open and willing to take a different look. Be open and willing to take a different look.

Another client, Phil, grew up in the ghetto. He had many stepfathers, drugs were a way of life, and brushes with the law were not unusual. He started applying himself after a particularly rough patch and in his mid-twenties, developed a very successful business. He never attended college but learned through his experience, trial and error. He, like the gentleman I just spoke about, worked with high-end clients. Phil's clients liked him, and he was invited to parties at their homes, but he felt very insecure going as he didn't have a college degree, and his upbringing seemed like it was from another planet compared to his clients. I shared with him that my most successful clients did not have college degrees (this is true). They started early with something they loved and then went with it full bore. They didn't want to waste valuable time in college when they could be developing their businesses. I gave him some names he was familiar with, like Bill Gates and Steve Jobs and some other highly-successful people who never finished college. I highlighted how much more he had to grow to overcome his circumstances than someone born with a silver spoon in their mouth. Those born with a silver spoon are expected to go to college, and the money is there, it's a given. They have contacts in place even before they graduate. But to start from the ghetto, with no role models, contacts, or education, and build a highly-successful business, *that* is a successful individual. I reminded him that; rather than feeling "less than," he should feel super proud of himself for coming so far. He reframed by realizing he had succeeded in spite of his circumstances and without all the silver-spoon benefits.

I had a young couple where one of the husband's beefs was that his wife was grumpy in the morning. Neither he nor the kids could even talk to her for a couple of hours after she woke up. This created a very uncomfortable environment for everybody in the morning. She controlled the family with her mood. I asked her why she would do this to herself, let alone her family that she professed to care so much about. She answered, "I don't know, that's just who I am."

I said, "I'm not asking you to change who you are, I'm just asking you to change your behavior so you and your family can have a nice morning. You tell yourself a story about yourself, that you're grumpy in the morning, and then you believe the story to the detriment of both you and your family."

Of course, this is easy to change if you are *willing* to shift your perspective. And why wouldn't you be? Well, let's see, there might be some secondary gains (payoffs) going on here. If someone is resistant to shifting their perspective, there's usually an underlying story. Maybe I like the attention and power of being the centerpiece, with people tiptoeing around me with trepidation. Maybe it makes me feel in control.

Reframing is a powerful tool, quick and easy to use, but in no way should it be used to avoid more deep-seated problems that you really do have control over. For example, if your fourth marriage is breaking up, this isn't the time to say, "Great, this will give me a chance to be independent again." Though that may be true, four marriages that didn't work out indicate a pattern that deserves exploration. Otherwise, the fifth is just around the corner.

If you find yourself resistant to reframing, you may be one of those people who always see the glass half empty, then deeper issues need to be explored. This could be an unconscious defense against disappointment that is destined to become a self-fulfilling prophecy. It could be the result of repressed anger. Whatever the cause, if left unresolved, a life of bitterness and resentment awaits. Remember, we are always choosing. We have a choice in how we interpret things. We take responsibility for our lives with each and every decision we make, and if we're smart about it, we decide what to think.

Covid-19 gave us a perfect opportunity to reframe, though many didn't use it. The news provided a running negative commentary and many allowed themselves to slide into despair. But did you notice how a few people used it as an opportunity to read more, to get closer to their families, their spouses, to get projects done that they never seemed to have time for? Others became depressed and anxious, fretting about what the future may hold. You can see that each of these perspectives created particular feelings: the first, feelings of closeness, efficacy, and gratitude; the second, feelings of fear and despair.

We recently bought a house in Sedona. We knew the size and location was perfect for an Airbnb and for us to enjoy the property now and then when we had time. The seller drove a hard bargain, holding firm way over the appraised value. We knew the location was perfect for us so we bought it anyway. I found myself lamenting that we paid so much over the appraised value, creating negative emotions. When I realized this, I was able to reframe the purchase in a positive light. It doesn't really matter what we paid; as an AirBnb, the property pays for itself; and we enjoy our time there immensely. Besides that, we love improving a property, and it has given us a fun project to work on. Changing my perspective, I now have only good feelings regarding this purchase.

Many in their golden years resist new technologies (me included!) and become almost phobic, leaving them with negative feelings of inadequacy and of being "left behind." Instead of resisting new technologies, try reframing them. Think of new technologies as brain exercises designed to keep your brain young and active. This will result in good feelings of competence and the feeling of being "current." Reframing not only results in better feelings, but it is also a prelude to better choices.

Try this: Take the next five negative things that come up in your life and reframe them in a positive way. Turn the lemons into lemonade.

Notice how your feelings change.

This is so much fun and so challenging, you might just decide to do it for the rest of your life!

Chapter 6

Focus

Focus is the ability to narrow your field of vision, thereby increasing your power. Think of a powerful river. The Colorado River, which runs through the Grand Canyon, runs fast and smooth when it has a wide berth, but when the rocks and cliffs crowd it into a narrow path, the enormous power of water building transforms it into rapids.

Ever hear a superstar athlete describe what it was like when he/she made the great play or won the grueling race? Often they'll say, "The world faded from my view, all I could see was the goal, it was like I was in slow motion with superhuman energy."

How about a scientist that has worked on a problem 24/7 and then goes to sleep and wakes up with the solution? Can you remember a time when you might have wanted a new house or an exotic vacation, and you couldn't think of anything else? You were obsessed with it. Then voilà! Like magic, you found yourself living in that new house or going on that great vacation. How about when you obsessed about what you *didn't want* (excess weight, for example), and it became a constant companion?

Focus allows energy to build until there is enough energy to flip into a new orbit; you want to make sure it's the orbit you want.

Speaking of focus, let me tell you about a dream I had many years ago. A man in a hooded white robe came to me in a dream, I couldn't see his face, and he asked me if I would like to learn how to become invisible. I thought for a minute, hmmm, then I said, "No," as I thought I might abuse that ability and eavesdrop on people. He began to slowly fade away. But then I thought, wait a minute, if I could learn to become invisible, then the inverse would also be true, I could learn how to make things visible. Materialize things, right? I quickly said, "Wait, yes," and the white-robed man faded in once again.

He drew two triangles, one on top of the other like an hourglass, the points of each triangle touching in the middle. He pointed to the top triangle and said, "This is the invisible," then he pointed to the bottom triangle and said, "This is the visible. And the point in the middle that connects them is focus."

I asked him his name, and he said, "Ethos."

I looked it up; ethos means "the essential characteristic of something." Little did I know that this was my first introduction to quantum mechanics, the new physics.

Interestingly, about six months later, my friend Neil called. He had heard an advertisement on the radio about some spiritual guy from Santa Fe, giving a talk at the Downtown Seattle Sheraton. Stuart Wilde was his name, and in the middle of his talk, he told us about a dream he had, in which some people came to him in a dream with a diagram. They drew two triangles with the points meeting in the middle; only it was sideways, like a bowtie. They pointed to one triangle and said, "That's the immaterial." Then they pointed to the other triangle and said, "That's the material." Different words, same story. Then Stuart Wilde said, "I never did get what the middle point was."

As you can imagine, the hair on the back of my neck went up. In spite of myself (there were two hundred people in the room), I raised my hand and shared that I had also gotten that message in a dream, but the diagram was upright, like an hourglass, and the robed man told me the middle point was focus. "That would make sense," Stuart said, and the room went silent while we all took in the implications of the two of us having the exact same dream experience with the exact same teaching.

Ethos came to me again some years later in a dream to reiterate the point. (*And I do mean* the *point!*) I guess he thought I needed a rebooting. He showed me the diagram again and pointed to the middle point of the two triangles, touching, and said, "This is like a laser."

Well, this was years ago, and I kind of knew about a laser, but I wasn't 100 percent sure how it worked, so I called my tennis partner who happened to be a physics professor. He explained that a laser is two mirrors with light going back and forth between them, faster and faster. *Coherent bits of light!* In other words, focus. Focused intention is the name of the game in this life, and modern physics bears this out. Einstein came along with $E = mc^2$. He showed mathematically that energy and matter are convertible. *And focus is the way to convert.*

In my early twenties, I was overweight. I'm only 5 feet 3 inches, and I weighed 123 lbs. That might not sound like a lot, but I have a small frame, and I am small-boned. When I saw a picture of myself on vacation with a couple of friends, I was horrified—I had no neck! This fat face was just balancing on top of my pudgy body.

For a few years, I obsessed about losing this weight, but to no avail. I could lose it all right, but before I knew it, I put it right back on. I must have lost and gained that weight ten times. My abject failure pushed me to try a different approach. I told myself I was not going to be fat *and* unhappy. If I couldn't lose the weight, I could at least choose to be happy, no matter what. I decided my focus would be to get healthy. I cut out a picture of a slim body that I liked, with my face pasted on top (at an earlier time when my face was not fat!), and I put it on the refrigerator door. I then set out to plan three healthy meals a day, with three healthy snacks. I shopped for the week, everything was down on paper, so there was no room for "winging it." Because of the consistent timed meals and snacks, I could always look forward to eating something in a few hours. Over time my addiction to eating unhealthy food just fell away, and I no longer had that "drive" to be eating. Concurrently, since my focus was on health and not on dieting, I began to exercise. Jogging was just getting popular, so I started to jog. Gradually, the weight began to fall off effortlessly and has stayed off ever since. Having a "healthy" focus is expansive, opening the door to many things and opportunities. A "losing weight" focus is constricting, focusing on what you don't want. It's a bummer to even think about.

Lucas was a client in his early thirties who embraced self-examination. Through his self-exploration, he became aware that he had muted his masculine energy as a result of being molested at a young age. With this awareness, Lucas then directed his energy toward getting in touch with and reinvigorating his masculine self. He read *The Superior Man* by David Deida. He started meditating and working with energy, and he began doing fifty burpees a day without fail. With Lucas's intense focus, his masculine power began to ignite, and he felt more in control of his life and his expression. I watched as even his body began to change to reflect his new self. This newfound power created by his focus and determination started attracting new opportunities and avenues of expression. It catapulted him into that man he had imagined. To this day, Lucas continues to learn, grow, and expand. I expect more great things for him in the future as he continues to put in the time and effort to make his dreams come true.

We are always creating our lives, but all too often, it's *unconscious* creating. Conscious creating is a result of focused intention. "Out of thin air" is a metaphor for making something visible from the invisible. It seems like magic, but really, it's just understanding how the universe works. You don't have to take anybody's word for it. In fact, I encourage you not to. It's better to see for yourself by experimenting. In my practice, I am often amazed when someone talks about the partner they have. I have them make a list of qualities, characteristics, and values they want in a partner, and sometimes, out of a twenty-item list, their partner may have only three or four items. And sometimes the qualities their partners do have are not the most important ones. Really? How did they choose that partner? The answer is they chose unconsciously. When I ask clients to make a list of the things they want in a partner and to consciously refer to that list, they are capable of screening people before they get emotionally involved. This saves a lot of time and heartbreak. Spending more time on the front end screening a partner saves having to work through problems on the back end. That's why many companies now do credit checks on prospective employees. A credit check will tell them if a prospective employee is responsible and reliable, thus saving the company time and money training an individual, only to have to fire them and repeat the process with yet another employee.

Think of something in the past that you focused on intensely and it came to be. Like the above examples, think of one positive example and one negative example. Choose one thing that you would like to achieve and apply laser-like focus on it.

For specified periods (maybe every day), put your all into it and watch what happens. Be patient. These things sometimes take time. Energy needs to build and accumulate as you maintain your focus.

Chapter 7

Planning

Anticipating and planning our future creates a roadmap for fulfilling our desires and allows us to do the best we can to ward off unpleasant surprises. If we see trouble coming, we can take a different road. One of my good friends put safety rails in the bathrooms for when she and her husband got old and feeble. That's a good plan but not the sort of plan I'm interested in. I know I'm going to get old, but hopefully, I won't get feeble. And if I do, I can put the safety rails in then. At the very least, I will work very hard to avoid that. When Dean's ninety-year-old mother Yolanda was living with us, she had trouble with her legs. We took her to an excellent physical therapist, who told her, "You are almost past the point of no return. The muscles along your back have atrophied to such a point that if you don't immediately take steps to change this, you will be in a wheelchair."

Born in a generation in which exercise was not a part of daily life, it was a hit and miss for Yolanda. A year later, she was in a wheelchair.

That gave Dean and I another powerful motivation for maintaining our regular exercise routine. Isn't it interesting that many people very carefully plan their financial futures so they don't outlive their money? Yet the same people could be fifty pounds overweight, living with an unsatisfying relationship, or letting their brains atrophy. I was surprised to learn that being overweight is the number one factor in susceptibility to Covid-19.

I'd love to be one of those people who wake up in the morning, going, "Yeah, let's get out there and get some exercise!" But that's not me. However, planning for a healthy life is me, and that entails having an exercise routine. Many choose the easy way despite the horrendous consequences of disease as well as the soaring health costs.

Jonathan's wife passed away, and he found himself feeling isolated. All his friends were people he got together with as a couple. After his spouse died, though he still saw his friends, it was not the same. Circumstances forced him to create a different plan for his life.

Jonathan had to look inside himself and decide what would be beneficial for him now. He decided that he needed to be more social. He had to get out there more to fill his need for connection. After careful consideration, he sold the house he had shared with his wife for years and bought a house in a community of fifty-five and older that offered beaucoup activities for the residents. By partaking in some of these activities, Jonathan found himself engaged in life once more, easing the loneliness he experienced after his wife died. In time, he found a companion, and three years later, they were married.

Remember, planning is almost as much fun as doing. Even if the plans do not come to fruition, one idea leads to another. And when the plans do manifest, it's a thrilling feeling. I had just graduated, and I was ready to start my first internship. I needed to have a supervisor to practice, and I wanted to be paid. I didn't want to just *get* an internship, many unpaid. I wanted to *create* one. I fantasized how I could develop a practice that would be right for me. I wanted an accomplished supervisor whom I respected and I could learn from. I wanted independence and the ability to structure my own time. And, again, I wanted to get paid.

I chose a therapist who didn't take interns, but I made him an offer he couldn't refuse. I told him I would occupy his office on his days off and would pay him 50 percent of what I took in. I would get my own liability insurance as well as paying him for his supervision. The plan cost him nothing and, in fact, made him money while he wasn't using his office. When I met with him, he asked me if I expected him to funnel clients to me. I replied no, that I would cultivate my own clients. I remember him looking at me with interest. I suspect he was wondering how I might do this. But I had a plan. His office was located in a very dense business community. I went door-to-door with newly-printed cards. I walked into offices and told everyone who would listen I was an intern who was excellent at what I did and charged a discounted rate of only $50. Bit by bit, my practice started to grow, not just by my legwork, but also by referrals. And before we moved to the Palm Springs area, I had a thriving little practice. Seeing my planning come to fruition, just as I had imagined, gave me the confidence to know I could establish a practice in any area. What was in my mind was made manifest by my planning and execution. If I could do this in one area, common sense would indicate I could do it in another.

Mary was married to a raging narcissist. Not long after she married her wealthy husband, she gave up her career to become a stay-at-home mom and had two children. After sweeping her off her feet in the beginning of their relationship, her husband became increasingly controlling and difficult, and she feared the influence he had on the children, not to mention what she had to endure with his constant criticisms and sarcastic remarks. She was psychologically savvy, so she knew her husband was a narcissist. She knew he would become belligerent and vindictive when she broached the subject of divorce. She knew she would have to fight for every cent and that her husband would try to negatively influence the kids against her. This situation was daunting for this intelligent young woman, but with careful planning, she found her way. She had to have patience, bide her time, and lay out the plans for herself until the timing was right to execute. She rehearsed the plan in her mind many times, and one day she was able to execute her exit plan smoothly with a minimum of anxiety.

Reese's father tried to touch her inappropriately when she was just sixteen. She was in high school. She started planning. She knew she had to support herself, so she got a job after school. As soon as she saved up the money, she bought a beater car. Next, she found an older cousin who was willing to have her as a roommate. Still at home with her dad and stepmom, Reese started organizing her things. She decided what was necessary to take with her, what she could leave behind, and then she packed everything up neatly so it was ready to go. Finally, one day, when they were at work, she moved out stealthily and never looked back.

Sam was a man I worked with, who was very unhappy with his job. He had the ability to move up with his company, but he was disappointed in the quality of the work they put out, he found himself embarrassed. An expert artisan, he took great pride in what he produced, but the company had less stringent standards. "I have a wife and three kids to support, I can't just quit!"

"No," I said, "but you can make a plan for more fulfilling work that would express who you really are."

He got many accolades for his work, and there were many clients that requested only him. This showed he had a clientele for the type of workmanship that he provided. His company was volume-focused, while he was quality-focused. That's a mismatch that will never be reconciled and will be a constant source of frustration. Once he realized this, he put a careful plan together for a graceful exit from his company. He did it without experiencing financial hardship. Now working for himself, he makes more than he ever thought possible, and he hires only those who share his vision of a quality product.

It's important in the planning process to make sure our plans are *rooted in reality*, rather than wishful thinking. At one point in our lives, we contracted with a builder who built custom homes. We wanted a smaller home, no bigger than 2,400 square feet. He told us an interesting story. He said he used to build custom homes in Lake Arrowhead. Everyone one wanted a big five-bedroom, five-bath house for when the children and grandchildren all came to visit. Great fantasy, right? The reality was most of the kids and grandkids lived in other areas, and they also had very busy lives. He told us a lot of the people he built for, realizing that their fantasy was not going to materialize, then contracted him to build something on a much smaller scale.

Richard is a client who's in a very unhappy relationship. He's been with his spouse for close to twenty years. He loves his wife dearly but realizes he has never gotten his needs met by her. He's tried many different approaches with his wife, but she's just not that interested in meeting his needs, though they are not unreasonable.

This is quite a dilemma: You love the person, but your needs are not being met. If the person didn't change in therapy or refused to even go, then chances are nothing will change. If you want to have a fulfilling life, you've got to go. I love that song by Paul Simon called "Fifty Ways to Leave Your Lover." This is the refrain: "Hop on the bus, Gus. Make a new plan, Sam. No need to be coy, Roy. Just set yourself free."

Relief comes from having the courage to move on when we're unhappy.

But first, we put together a plan.

The plan is the well-thought-out blueprint that gives us security. Again, good and realistic planning on the front end, forestall disasters on the backend. Make planning fun. Make it a challenge. Planning requires knowing ourselves, actually taking the time to figure out what makes us happy and what kind of expression we need. Maybe some of our plans don't work out, but that's okay, it's a starting point. We can always pivot and go in a different direction. The idea is to get the juices flowing.

What are three goals you currently have? Put a plan together to achieve each one.

Remember, the plan doesn't have to be set in stone. You can change it, if you like or if the situation changes.

Chapter 8

Simplicity

Simplicity is a stunning mistress. If you allow her to have her way, she will reveal untold riches. She will lead you to the Rio Abajo Rio (the river beneath the river) where true expansiveness lies. Why? Because you are no longer encumbered. Contemplate simplicity, look deeply, it will be worth your time.

It's human nature to strive to become more, to express more. In our culture and most of the world, that drive is channeled into acquisition. Acquisition is not bad, not at all. But at best, it temporarily assuages the internal longing to be more. It can even lead us down a rabbit hole to nowhere. I remember a quote from David Geffen of the Dream Team, "Those that think money will make them happy have obviously never had it."

In the traditional Japanese tea ceremony, only one object of art is on the table at any given time. You can truly appreciate the piece of art without distraction. This enables you to go deep into the nature of the object, rather than skimming over the surface of many objects in a half-knowing or shallow way. Deep is expansive, wide is compulsive.

Contrast this with a modern Christmas Day. Kids unwrap gift after gift. They are so anxious to get to the next one that they don't even stop to examine what they've already unwrapped. I remember my friend John telling me the story of when he took his kids over to his parents for Christmas. There were so many presents under the tree that halfway through opening them, the grandkids just got up and went down to the basement to play.

In design school, it's called "less is more." The idea being that negative space is as important as positive space. You want to be able to "breathe" in a space as well as in life. Imagine a hoarder, where every square inch of space is taken up with something. Every time you turn around it's a cacophony of items bombarding your senses. Now imagine being on an isolated beach on a deserted island, hearing just the soft lapping of the waves. It doesn't take much to imagine the difference in how you *feel*.

When I lived in Santa Barbara, my friend Bob and his wife flew in to attend a workshop given by a man named Roehner. Roehner worked mostly with doctors and dentists, and he helped them revamp their lives and their businesses so that they were more successful in every way. I was invited by Bob and his wife to be their guest for a day. The day I attended, Roehner asked his clients to go through their lives with a fine-tooth comb, every single object, large or small, *everything* they owned, down to the bobby pins. With each item, they were to ask themselves, "Does this add meaning to my life?"

If the answer was no, the item was discarded.

I remember one couple who had a house full of valuable antiques that had been passed down for generations. Roehner asked them if they enjoyed the furniture. Turns out, they hated antique furniture but kept it because they thought they should. It was worth a lot of money for one thing, and then there was the idea that they were keeping the family legacy alive, so to speak, by passing it down. It was a relief to this couple to actually let go of these items that added nothing to their life and actually bogged them down. The last thing I remember Roehner saying was, "You should clean out your closet twice a year, it's a spiritual experience."

I was already in the habit of doing that every fall and spring, but I didn't extend it into every single thing I owned down to the bobby pins. I do now, and Roehner's right—it truly is a spiritual experience.

I remember a client of mine, furious with her husband for questioning her handbag purchases. She asked me, "How many handbags do you have?" I replied that I had one for winter and one for summer. She was aghast. "Really? You only have two handbags?"

She looked crestfallen. I think she was confident that she would find agreement from me that every lady should have handbags matching every outfit. And that would be fine if that made her happy. For me, that would complicate life, meaning with every outfit, I would be changing all my things into a different bag. I'd rather invest my time and energy where the return is greater. I have a good friend who has lots of beautiful jewelry that she changes on a daily basis. I love to see what she's wearing on any given day. I wear the same jewelry that I love every day. There's no right or wrong here. If it adds value to your life, then great. If you're doing something by rote or following some social program established by who-knows-who, you might want to reevaluate.

Dean and I bought a big house when his elderly mother came to live with us. We wanted a separate wing so we could maintain our privacy, and so could she. We put a fifty-foot lap pool in the backyard with a huge jacuzzi and beautiful palm trees. We planted citrus trees on the side and had a lovely rose garden as well as an herb garden. After three years, Dean's mother, Yolanda, moved into an assisted-care facility. Even before she left, most of our time was spent in the great room or the bedroom. The house was a lot to maintain, and we had to have people around to do it: gardeners, housekeepers, window washers. Things would break. We employed plumbers and electricians. I remember coming home from a two-week vacation and our sidewalk had collapsed caused by an underground pipe bursting. It was *busy*.

Remember, everything you own owns a piece of you.

Brent, one of my wealthier clients, lives in an exclusive country club in a gorgeous home that looks like an Italian villa. It took four months to paint the outside of his house, and then there's the inside. Window washers come every month. Workmen, gardeners, and housekeepers are always there working. Like painting the Golden Gate bridge, as soon as they get to the end of the bridge, they begin all over again. This is what it takes to maintain an estate. *More cows, more responsibility.* If it adds value to your life, then okay. If it doesn't, make a different choice.

Let's expand this even further. It's not just about objects in your life, it's also about people, events, lifestyle, routines, and the like. Let's talk about friends and family. Ever had lifelong friends or family members who just don't do it for you anymore? In some cases, they actually drag you down. My client Joe had a horrendous adult son who was in his thirties. The son was belligerent and demanding, guilting his successful dad into bailing him out of various fixes he got himself into. Joe tried everything to get his son on his feet. He bailed him out of things, he bought him a car, he found a job for him (he couldn't keep it), he paid for therapy (the son didn't go), etc. All the while, the son is blaming his dad for everything and playing the victim card. I asked Joe why he would continue a relationship that was nothing but a drain of resources, mentally, emotionally, psychologically, and financially. "Because he's my son."

I have heard this type of refrain over and over in the years that I've practiced psychotherapy. "She's my oldest friend."

"She's my mother. What do you want me to do?"

"I've known him since high school. I can't desert him when he's going through a bad time (one of many bad times)."

"Blood is thicker than water."

The funniest line I ever heard around this "family" thing was a client in her forties who had married into a big Italian family. She said, "All I ever hear about is family, family, family. We all have to stick together. Blood is thicker than water. But all of them hate each other and are constantly running around talking smack behind each other's backs."

We had some longtime friends whom we loved, and over the years, we had had a lot of fun with them. In time, the wife's drinking problem became increasingly tiresome for us. She became louder and louder during dinners in restaurants, she ruined parties by becoming falling-down drunk, and after a certain point in the evening, it was clear that she was "not there." We were honest and let her know how this behavior made us feel, but nothing changed. Unfortunately, her husband was not willing to establish boundaries around her drinking. Did we stop loving her? Of course not. But did we want to continue to subject ourselves to her behavior? Absolutely not. Though they were old, beloved friends, we let the friendship go as it was no longer enjoyable.

With Joe and his adult son mentioned above, after a lot of therapy, Joe was able to cut his son loose and begin to appreciate that he could choose what kind of life he wanted, and the insane dynamic with his adult son wasn't in it. Simplifying your life also entails letting go of individuals who do not enhance it.

How about simplicity in communicating? Honesty is elegant and simple. Lying or obfuscating the truth is complicated. Isn't it great to communicate with a person who is truthful and straightforward? No games, no guessing, no wondering if they're just saying this but they might mean that. Marsha told me she loves her mother-in-law as she always knows where she stands with her. If they are in the area and they ask if a visit might be possible, her mother-in-law will say whatever is the truth. "No, that doesn't work for me today," or "Yes, sounds good."

Some people would just say yes because they think they should and then end up resenting the visitors, maybe even being crabby. With this mother-in-law, everyone knows what the deal is. Ever say yes when you mean no and then you feel angry afterwards? Complicated.

I remember visiting some friends in Albuquerque. We all met for brunch, and afterwards, we were going to meet up and go to a museum. All through brunch, I felt an undercurrent of something going on between the two of them. It was like a silent, unspoken fight. As we tried to determine a time to meet later, they went back and forth in polite disagreement. I finally made it easy for them as I couldn't tolerate the two conversations at the same time (the spoken one and the silent one). I said, "I'm heading back to the hotel. Call me when, and if, you'd like to meet."

I'm pretty sure they had a bang-up fight as soon as I departed. They could have just said, "We're having a rough time right now. Can we just call it off today? Or let us call you after we sort ourselves out."

They could have called even before we headed off to brunch and said, "This isn't a good day for us," and all of us would have had a better day.

When people say, "The truth will set you free" they're 100 percent right. The truth *will* set you free. It's so simple, almost too simple, many people completely miss it.

Here's another example: Jason, a young, intelligent, good-looking client of mine, with many wonderful attributes, started dating a girl he really fell for. She told him that he was attractive and that, on paper, he had all the qualities she wanted in a man. He said, "If that's true, why not see where this goes?"

She explained that she was working on herself currently, but who knows what the future will bring? I felt she was not being completely honest with my client, that she was keeping him hopeful in the wings, while he provided her with security. I explained to my client that he could have all the qualities she desired, but that didn't mean she was attracted to *him*. Chemistry is hard to explain. When you're hot, you're hot, and when you're not, you're not. This realization gave him the impetus to actually ask the right question: Are you attracted to *me*? I give this gal credit for answering honestly so he could be on his way rather than spending all his time with her in hopes that she may one day change her mind.

Simplicity of mind. What about the negative space inside your head? Is there any? Or is it just thinking, thinking, thinking, endless yammering away about who-knows-what? Have you ever noticed how you will endlessly narrate what you already know? Some experts say we think sixty thousand to eighty thousand thoughts per day. Yikes! That's a lot of thinking *and a lot of energy spent*. Can't say that will lead to a lot of peace and serenity. Dean caught himself counting his strokes while in the swimming pool. For what? He just wanted to be present and enjoy the water, but before he knew it, the "monkey mind" showed up. Have you ever tried *not* to think? Not as easy as it sounds. There are techniques, however, that move you in that direction: meditation is one of these; any kind of art, writing, painting, cooking, gardening; flow states created by sports like running, surfing, skiing, swimming; tai chi or qi gong; things that you do where you're not thinking. A lot of us live our lives in our heads, and we rarely experience flow states that are exhilarating and expanding. Flow states are also restorative, by the way. Thinking can be exhaustive, you just don't realize it. The prefrontal cortex, or neocortex, is the brain's executive function. It's like the CEO of you. It's very important for many things, but we don't want to let it become a tyrant.

Because Dean and I have a lot going on in our lives, one of our biggest challenges is keeping things simple, not filling the day with the endless things that need to get done, prioritizing, and creating space. If you make simplicity an ongoing goal, it's easier to keep life in balance. Life shouldn't be just a series of tasks. There needs to be time for just "being." Watching a sunrise, seeing the cats at play, enjoying a good book, all these things are restorative.

I'm reminded of a keen observation of Soren Kierkegaard, a Danish philosopher in the 1800s. He observed, "The simple man on his way home after work is wondering what's for dinner. The complex man on his way home from work is debating the complexities and the imponderables of life. The enlightened man on his way home from work is wondering what's for dinner."

I love this quote, and I'm going to include it in a cookbook someday as it's not only a philosophy for life but also a philosophy for cooking. Here's a great example: Dean is a fabulous cook, and we have a favorite duck dish that can be done in an hour and a half. One Thanksgiving he wanted to try a French duck recipe that had numerous ingredients and required various layers of work. He was in the kitchen for over four hours, and the finished product? Not nearly as good as the duck dish that takes one and a half hours.

Over the years of trying different things in the kitchen, I've seen this time and again. Good, fresh, organic ingredients, with simple recipes, produce the tastiest meals. The more complicated the recipes, the less likely a mouth-watering result. And yet many people have it in their minds that if it's more complicated, the result has to be better. Our favorite cheese is Reggiano parmesan from Italy. It's the same simple recipe for over six hundred years, a classic that can't be beat.

The Bauhaus design group of the 1920s had a simple philosophy: Form follows function. They created simple designs with clean lines that are just as sought after today as they were in the last century. They're timeless. You will still see the designs in high-end houses, offices, and hotels.

Our choices provide us with simplicity in our lives or lead us into chaos. This point was driven home to me when, as an intern, Dean and I were running an anger management group. We had eighteen men who were mandated to attend as a result of spousal abuse. The meetings were held in Desert Hot Springs, the northwest end of the valley. There was a time when one out of every three people who resided in Desert Hot Springs were felons. Our group met once a week, and we worked with the guys to develop new coping skills rather than resorting to violence.

At one particular time, we had a new person in the group who was just out of prison and on parole. Everybody in the group had issues, but I could feel that this guy was really dangerous. He was a huge guy with giant arms, very intelligent, and an intensity that was palpable. He was talking about an incident he just had, and without giving the gory details, just suffice to say, it was ruthless. I was afraid of him, I knew there was nothing he wouldn't do if he felt like it. All eighteen guys are looking at me, waiting for me to comment. My mind was racing as I debated how I would respond to this man. This guy could squish me like a grape. He could be waiting by my car. But I'm here to do therapy, to try and help even this tortured soul. After a pregnant pause, I responded slowly. "It's just so complicated," meaning, the way he chose to live his life and the fixes he got himself into. To my relief, he answered, "I hear you," and gazed off into the distance as he took that in.

The next week, just before we started our meeting, three police cars converged to take him down with handcuffs, and we never saw him again. This man created the most chaotic life imaginable with his choices. This is an extreme example, but we can always back it down to what the rest of us do on a smaller scale if we are not mindful. We can become addicted to a stressful life, and peering into simplicity can help us see our way out.

Lots of things sound fun to me, and when I was younger, I would constantly overbook with things. Then I became exhausted, and even if things were fun, my fatigue robbed me of the enjoyment. Then I would do nothing for a while until I recovered. Then I would start all over again. It was like binge drinking. Recognizing that even too much fun isn't fun brings us back to simplicity. Our culture tells us more is "better" when, really, the opposite is often true. I'm reminded of what Vince Lombardi, the great football coach for the Green Bay Packers, said about fatigue: "Fatigue makes cowards of us all." Overbooking, overthinking, over-striving, all sap our energy and dilute the joy of life.

In today's busy world, let's talk about creating more time. The very young have no idea that time is a commodity. Anyone middle aged and beyond has experienced time flying by. Yet many waste their time in trivial pursuits. How much of your time do you spend on social media every day? How many hours do you waste surfing the Internet? What about watching the news, binge watching TV, or playing video games 24/7? How about eating up hours on the telephone with friends or family or mindless shopping for things you do not need? Simplicity also involves clearing out wasteful, useless activities that we use to zone out but take us away from our goals. Think of hours as dollars. Where are you spending them, and what is your return on investment?

What can you do right now to simplify your life?

Look at what areas of your life you could simplify to create space or time?

Choose one area to start. What's the plan? What can be eliminated and in what time frame? Envision how it would feel once done.

Chapter 9

Independent Thinking

Independent thinking means you think for yourself, instead of "What will my parents think?" "What will my children think?" "What will my spouse, my friends, my associates, my political party, my boss, my employees, my church fellows, my sports buddies think?"

There's an old Taoist saying that's really worth remembering: "Those who care what others think become their prisoners."

Isn't it true? I know it's hard to divorce oneself from the cultural and familial programming that we are all subject to, but it's that or becoming an automaton. Where is the happiness in that? You don't even know who you really are. Just being a collection of programs does not lead to an authentic life filled with creative energy and excitement. Have the courage to evaluate your thinking on an ongoing basis *to determine* whether it's what you think or whether you're modifying your thoughts and beliefs to fit in or to avoid disapproval or abandonment.

Or you just swallow what you hear wholesale and don't take the time to think things through.

I have a new young client Patricia, who is attending college. She's very smart and totally unhappy. She's a first-generation immigrant, born in this country. She's expected to make the family proud by, you guessed it, becoming a doctor, lawyer, or engineer. She is unhappy because she's been living a life that's not her own. Patricia wants the approval of her parents but doesn't want to sacrifice her authentic self in the process. She loves music and acting, and she has talent. Just thinking about letting go of others' expectations of her and imagining her preferred future lifted Patricia's depression. When we deny our hearts to please whoever, depression and emptiness are the result.

Here's an example of buying into political correctness because we don't have the courage to call it BS. I was down at the pool doing laps when a new gentleman in our community asked me if I was still doing the "Wim Hof breathing method" that I told him about. I answered yes and asked him if he was still doing it. He said no as he didn't have a partner like I have to keep me in line. The next day I'm out at the pool reading a book, and this gentleman asked if he could speak with me. I said yes, and he went on to say he misspoke and would like to apologize for saying I had a partner to keep me in line. Really?

Political correctness had cowed this wonderful man into thinking he had offended me in some way by saying I had a partner to keep me in line. I knew his joking intentions. I was in no way offended. And even if he had personally meant it as an insult, who cares? Ever heard that old saying "Sticks and stones will break my bones, but words will never hurt me"?

That saying was designed to toughen us up; to be warriors, not victims; to carry our strength on the inside rather than reacting to every little thing on the outside.

There's a vast psychological difference between a victim and a warrior. Assuming the "victim stance" in any situation has enormous negative psychological and often physical implications. Now we have all been victimized in one way or another sometime in our lives, but that doesn't mean we have to embrace the victim role. That's a choice. It may feel good in the moment, allowing you to feel sorry for yourself or garner sympathy from others. It may cause you to feel morally superior.

But once you realize that accepting the victim role cripples you by shutting down your personal growth and disempowering you, you might want to make a different choice. Beware of anyone or any group that encourages you to be a victim.

I've worked with many clients who were single parents or divorced at a later stage in life, and they are terrified of upsetting their adult children. If they're not careful, they will alter their lives to keep peace or acceptance in their relationships with their children. Many children (young or adult) work tirelessly to dissuade a suitor of one of their parents. Sometimes it's about the money. If mother or father remarries, then the financial picture could change. Sometimes they just do not want to adjust to a new situation. They don't want to share. If your kids are interested in anything other than your happiness, then it's time to rethink the relationship. We are the only ones who can procure happiness for ourselves, and if that means disappointing others, *even your kids*, then so be it. I'm not talking about being inconsiderate or infringing on other people's rights. I'm talking about having the courage to stand up for what you think and believe and self-activating to get what you want in this life. And if you haven't done it up until now, no problem, this is a skill you can learn, and you'll love the way it feels.

I started meditating in 1971. Other than my own personal therapy, it is the single most beneficial and life-changing thing I've done. But in 1971, it was considered "weird" and "fringe." Friends would look at me sideways and laugh. I knew people were probably laughing and talking about me behind my back, but it didn't matter because I knew it was beneficial. Now the benefits of meditation are well-known. It's discussed on daily talk shows. Major corporations have free classes teaching their employees how to meditate. A plethora of books, apps, and podcasts are available. If I had allowed what others thought to influence me, I never would have achieved the wonderful benefits I continue to experience.

Back in the '60s, there was only one health food store/restaurant in Las Vegas. Our friend Frankie, also a meditator, was a loyal patron, and his friends teased him mercilessly for what they thought were far-out practices. Frankie has outlived many of his friends and is healthy, active, and strong as an ox in his eighties. He thought for himself and ended up getting the last laugh.

I have had many clients who want to try something new, but they're afraid their partner or friends will ridicule them, and often they're right. A man wants to learn the tango, A woman wants to learn to shoot or box. Another person wants to explore spirituality or art. So? Are we going to let what other people think stop us? Once more, courage is needed to go after your heart's desires, no matter what anybody thinks. When we thwart our heart's desires, we say hello to depression.

I remember in the old days that a woman would bite her tongue so as not to be thought of as unladylike. Or how about this: a man would hide his real feelings for fear of looking like a wuss. Two people can be in a relationship and have absolutely no idea of how their partner really feels and thinks because of the roles each individual thinks they should play. That's a complete lack of intimacy, and it's not just in the old days. There are variations of this going on in my office all the time. What if we were just true to ourselves and accepted that maybe everybody is not going to like it? *Mmmm* . . . Freeing! I read a book once in which the author wisely said, "A third of the people will like you, a third of the people won't like you, and a third of the people are indifferent."

You are never going to win them all, so forget about it and live your life *according to you.*

Critical thinking is not just necessary, it's also exciting. But it does take courage. Maybe that's why it's exciting. Sometimes you have to stand alone, like when the mob of political correctness comes after you or when the medical community tells you what's best. I have the BRCA1 gene, which is an aggressive cancer gene. Many on my mother's side have died of cancer, including my mother who died at forty-seven. I was told I really needed to have a double mastectomy and a hysterectomy to survive. Perhaps that will prove to be true, but I'm willing to take my chances before bombarding my body with invasive surgeries, toxic chemicals, and radiation. And by the way, I don't have cancer! When I tally up the price tag for the surgeries, as well as the courses of radiation and chemo, I see why the doctors put on a full-court press.

There was a book written in the '50s titled *Rules for Radicals* by Saul Alinsky. It was basically about stealthily overthrowing an existing government structure. One of the methods was to indoctrinate unsuspecting minds. Alinsky called them "useful idiots".

I was surprised when a student who graduated from Western Washington State had neither heard of nor read the book. It was not included in the political science curriculum, even though it's been used as the playbook of some presidential campaigns. An agenda is exposed not just by what is presented, but also by what is omitted. If we don't think for ourselves, we are easy prey for others who don't always have our best interests at heart.

Agendas are everywhere. That's why it's so important for us to use our common sense. Independent thinking is the difference between living other people's lives and or living your own. It's the difference between being a sovereign individual rooted in reality and a "useful idiot" that just buys the current narrative.

Because critical thinking keeps your brain active and forces you to come to your own conclusions, it builds esteem and confidence.

Go deep. Be honest with yourself. Check to see if your values and opinions are truly yours or the result of a "program." ·

If you find some values and opinions are really a result of programming, do the self-exploratory work to come up with what's truly yours.

Chapter 10

Discipline

Some people think discipline is a dirty word. Nothing could be further from the truth. Discipline is an absolute choice, and it's your ticket to freedom. Discipline is magical in nature because once you create the settings, then it's as simple as following the yellow brick road to your goals.

I remember when I first got out of school, and I wanted to be "free." I traveled around with hardly any money, taking each day as it came and searching for adventure. Of course, having little money really curtailed what experiences I could partake in. My friend Greg, on the other hand, was disciplined and started working and planning his future as soon as he got out of college. Within a few years, he was traveling around the world with a friend of his because they had the money to do so.

Greg had a myriad of choices at his disposal and, I am sure, had much more exotic adventures than I was having at that time. I began to contemplate what freedom actually meant and what it would take to be really free. Discipline was the answer. I wasn't really free if I had limited choices, and if I didn't have discipline, my choices would remain limited. I started to look at discipline with new eyes, as a vehicle of opportunity. It wasn't restrictive. It opened up new vistas of possibility.

Discipline can turn your every action into solid gold. My client Paul was wound really tight and very reactive, especially in relationships. He was a great guy, yet because of this reactivity, many people who loved this man left him. I encouraged him to develop the discipline to start mastering his moods, to begin a meditation practice, and to develop a philosophy of glass half full rather than glass half empty. In about six months, Paul's energy was completely transformed.

He felt good, looked at the bright side of things, and was able to maintain a loving relationship.

After a year or so, I began to notice Paul's energy unraveling, the barrage of negative thoughts, the quarrels with his partner. "Are you doing your practice?" I asked.

"No," he replied.

I didn't really have to ask. I knew the answer already. His energy spoke volumes. For this man, the discipline of keeping up the practice we had established was the key for him to get the life he wanted. When he fully realized this, he disciplined himself to implement his practice once again. And things got good again.

Sarah, a client in her twenties, hated her body. "How much are you willing to do to change your body?" I asked her.

"Anything," she answered.

That's the kind of answer a therapist/life coach wants to hear because that shows determination and commitment, which, in turn, propels clients to success. We broke it down. We talked about what she ate, if she ever exercised, etc., all the things that go into creating a fit body. I asked her if she ever did any sports, and she said she wasn't athletic. I told her that telling herself she wasn't athletic was just a story she told herself and that she could change the story right here and now. I already knew the story wasn't true because she moved with fluidity. My guess was she'd tried different sports at school, not done that well at them (like all of us, until we put in the time and effort to become better—*discipline*), and then decided she just wasn't athletic.

One aspect of discipline is staying with something long enough to reap the benefits because, more often than not, it takes a while. I told Sarah to choose a sport that was fun and exercised her whole body and become a master of it. She chose tennis. Then we talked about what she ate, and we restructured her eating habits and food choices. Last, we discussed how working with a trainer can reshape our bodies. She got a trainer. In less than six months, she had a different body.

Because the goal was so important to her, she was able to develop the discipline to establish a three-pronged approach to get the body she wanted, and she got it. Think of all the famous bodybuilders that you hear of. They didn't start out with great bodies. Discipline was Sarah's key to getting the body she loved.

Everywhere I look today I see overweight children and teenagers. What do you think happens to overweight kids? They are teased, ridiculed, can't get girlfriends or boyfriends, can't do sports, develop diseases like diabetes, and they hate themselves. What parents would want this for their child? But parents are the models for eating behaviors and limits. So why would you even have soda in your house? Or any other food that is unhealthy? Once again, having personal discipline as a parent provides a model for your children. Teaching kids that discipline is a powerful characteristic to develop opens up possibilities for them. Giving kids limits helps them develop discipline and overcome instant gratification. We want our kids to have a great life, and discipline is a key component in making that happen.

Think of Tom Brady. In 2000, he was the thirty-third pick in the sixth round of the NFL draft. How did he go from last pick to "the best quarterback in history"? He worked his ass off. The story is he worked out like a madman, on and off season. He studied endless films of his team playing as well as the films of his upcoming opponents. I heard that after every game, you could find him going over the film of the game and noting what the team could have done better and where some of the weaknesses were. He put everything he had into developing his skill, and presto! He got the goods.

I once worked with an intelligent gentleman we'll call William. William struggled to find a meaningful career for himself. A meaningful career to him meant being creative, contributing to the world, and making a good living. Though he yearned for creative expression, he lacked the discipline to set the stage for it to happen. Plans we put together had no teeth as he was unable to follow through and accomplish his goal. Since he had inherited money (parents, remember this!), there was no impetus for him to design and implement a plan. Life threw out many distractions, as it always does, and unconsciously, he allowed himself to get caught up in them, buying his own rationalizations. Though he did not feel good about himself, he was unwilling to change his behavior.

Establishing self-discipline would have enabled William to get to the other side and start developing esteem through efficacy. Good feelings about himself would have followed. Unconsciously, he was choosing feeling bad over feeling good. He had the intelligence and the knowledge but didn't put it into action; think static energy versus kinetic energy, potential versus activation. Self-activation is crucial in life to get what you want. However, no therapist/life coach can make someone do it. You must choose to do it yourself.

It takes discipline to create. It doesn't "just happen" like a lot of people think. You don't become a pro golfer, a great musician, a terrific accountant, a good anything without putting in your time. You don't get a great relationship without putting in your time. Or how about this: You don't create a happy life of enjoyment and satisfaction without putting in your time. In Malcolm Gladwell's book, *The Tipping Point*, he points out that successful people are willing to put in their time to get the results they want. He highlights many famous, successful people we all know, who many would say are just "lucky," and then illustrates what they had to do to finally achieve their success. Malcolm says ten thousand hours is the tipping point. Twyla Tharp, one of America's great choreographers, says it's Pavlovian. If you follow the routine (discipline), you get a creative pay off.

I have a friend who is in very good shape but has back issues. He tweaked his back, and his wife told me he walked bent over like an old man for six months. Finally, he found a doctor who gave him a series of stretches, which he did religiously, and his back completely recovered. A couple of years later, he had another severe bout with his back. I asked him if he was still doing his stretches, and chagrined, he said no. He knew if he had continued to do the stretches, he would not be in this predicament. But this is human nature, isn't it? We all have to be watchful of letting our discipline fall away, or we will return to our comfort zone.

Ian has adult epilepsy. I told him about the tremendous success with the ketogenic diet. He tried it, and within two weeks, he stopped having seizures, and his brain fog subsided. The ketogenic diet is a bit of a challenge to maintain, so Ian fell off the wagon, so to speak, and the episodes and brain fogginess came back. In some cases, lack of discipline is related to "worthiness." This is what needs to be explored in therapy. Did he not feel worthy enough to be well?

Vicky was an unbelievably shy client. She was a successful doctor, but that hadn't required her to develop any social skills. She felt like no one liked her, but the truth was she had so much social anxiety that people could feel it, and it made *them* uncomfortable, so they pulled away. You could feel it in the air. As with any phobia, it must be faced and worked through. And what does it take? Yep, that's right—*discipline.* I suggested she go to Toastmasters or the Dale Carnegie classes on public speaking and also that she read *How to Win Friends and Influence People* by Dale Carnegie (an old classic worth its weight in gold).

She joined Toastmasters, which she attended every week, and she was required to give speeches on an ongoing basis. In the beginning, it was absolute torture. Vicky brought her speeches into her sessions with me, and she went over them multiple times, filled with terror. Gradually, by forcing herself to face her fears, she began to get comfortable. Soon she couldn't wait to get up and give a speech. Her speeches were creative, and the other attendees loved hearing what she would come up with. She was overwhelmed with admiration. Her discipline of not giving up and forcing herself to do something that was extremely uncomfortable gave her a new view of herself that was transformative and had everlasting value.

How about the discipline needed to leave a toxic relationship? Sometimes a person still loves someone but knows the relationship is toxic. Or maybe they are just not getting their needs met. It takes discipline to look at the facts, make the decision, and to not just move on but to stay away. One might feel the immediate relief of going back into the relationship, but they only prolong the painful process of separating eventually. I knew of a couple that remarried three times. And the marriage fell apart anyway. Imagine if they'd had the discipline to redirect their energies after the first round.

How about the discipline to always tell the truth? To always have a voice? To eradicate negative thoughts in our head or criticism of others? The discipline to be kind, to not judge? To stay in the present moment? To manage our food, our health, our communication, our finances, our boundaries? I could go on and on. Discipline, or the lack of, permeates all areas of our lives. It's best to make it our friend and purposely develop it, knowing it provides freedom on every level.

In what areas are you undisciplined?

What do you lose in each area as a result of being undisciplined?

Take each area and write down what disciplinary actions would shore that area up.

Notice how much closer you feel to your ultimate goal in each area just by imagining taking the required actions.

Chapter 11

Meaning

One of my favorite existential psychologists is Irving Yolum. He talks about his clients always asking, "What is the meaning of life?"

Good question, right? Wouldn't we all like to know? This is what philosophers have pondered forever. Yalom told his clients that the meaning of life is what they give it. I'm sure some people resisted that response. Why? Because that puts the onus on the person asking the question. In other words, we have to take the responsibility to find our own meaning. Rather than being passive and waiting for an answer, enlist your own imagination and creativity to come to your own conclusions.

This can be a point of departure or discovery. If you find yourself saying, "Is that all there is?" then you have some definite work to do. It's time to do some self-evaluation.

What has meaning at one stage of your life may not have meaning at another stage, so it's important to be flexible and open to rediscovery.

Years ago I read a book titled *The Paradigm Shift*, and the author talked about when something loses its meaning for us, we tend to try and do more of the same thing. The problem is it doesn't work. I can relate. Years ago I had a resort shop that was enjoyable for a stretch of time, but after a while, I got sick of doing retail sales. A huge new mall was being built, and I decided to open a second shop. For a while, the creativity of designing the shop and buying for the new store was invigorating. But not long after I opened, I remember being in the new shop, thinking, *Here I am, doing retail sales again . . . just in a new location.*

We have to be honest with ourselves and evaluate what turns us on right *now*. It doesn't mean some things can't give us meaning throughout our lives. Spirituality is one of those things for me. It just means sometimes we have to recalibrate and find new meaning. If we don't, stagnation is the result. To readjust, we have to go deep, we have to take some time with ourselves to figure things out, and we have to be okay with not knowing until we know. Brain studies now tell us that the brain craves certainty. Ambiguity (or uncertainty) actually creates activity in the amygdala. The amygdala filters information to determine the threat level, while decreased activity in the ventral striatum diminishes our reward response. We have to override these physiological responses to provide the time and space to figure out what we need currently.

Jeff is a client who has done many different things in his life, but now he gets meaning from rescuing and caring for animals. He feels like this will make him happy for the rest of his life. This may or may not be true, but either way, he can make a different choice later. What's important is that we stay aware, and if we find our lives devoid of meaning, we change it.

Robert is a highly-successful client who is retired and is now looking for new meaning. His spouse passed away last year. He had a wonderful career, but it ran its course, and now he wants something different. Money is not an issue. He has the money to do whatever he wants. He's in limbo, trying to figure out what has meaning for him now. In this stage, we have to be patient with ourselves. We have to welcome being in limbo, though it feels uncomfortable. It feels as if the sand beneath our feet is shifting. But we don't want to impulsively dive into something just to alleviate the uncomfortable feeling. This is when it's important to stay the course, look within, and really explore yourself deeply.

I see people whose careers have lost meaning for them. The careers have become drudgery, and the side effect of this is exhaustion. Feeling tired all the time can reveal a lack of meaning in one's life, a need to shift gears. Sometimes it's hard to shift gears. You have a house payment and a car payment, and you're paying for the kids' college. Your good income makes all that possible. How can you let that go? Well, here's the thing: Life goes by. If you're unhappy, that's a sad state of affairs. And the responsibility is yours. You may think you're doing it for the kids, but you're teaching your kids that it's okay to be unhappy without taking action to make any changes. I'm not saying to dump your job without having a plan. What I see, more often than not, is that when clients are courageous enough to make changes when they are not happy, life blooms in an extraordinary way. You see, when we are happy and we enjoy life, we are far more productive and creative. We have much more energy at our disposal.

Jerry was a man who spent his early years developing his business. He had relationships, but they were not a priority and, therefore, never deepened into something long lasting. When he was close to fifty, he recalibrated and decided he wanted someone in his life to be a long-term companion. His business provided meaning for him originally, and though it still did, meaning at this point required something additional. When he got in touch with this, it was not long after that he met a woman who fit the bill. Sometimes just realizing what we need creates the energetic space to find it.

Sharon was a woman who raised her kids, cooked and cleaned, went to games and swim meets, and all that held tremendous meaning for her. But by the time her youngest was in high school and the other kids were in college, she was adrift. She enjoyed her twenty years of raising kids, but she was glad they were almost over. She wanted to find something that had meaning for her currently. She realized that she and her husband had nothing in common, a point that was previously obfuscated by their busy lives. She decided to start her own business, something that had always interested her, and it began to flourish.

Energized by new meaning and excitement in her life, Sharon decided to tackle the other area of her life that was less than satisfying—her marriage. She and her husband loved each other, but they had grown apart. They came into therapy, willing to try and make their marriage work. They developed new communication skills and implemented new ways of creating intimacy in their marriage. Because this woman self-activated on every front when she found herself thinking, "Is that all there is?" she was able to recreate a successful, meaningful life for herself and find happiness.

I contrast this approach with my neighbor Stew. Whenever I see Stew, I say, "Hi, Stew, how are you?"

I continue to ask because it's a way of showing that I care, but it's always the same answer: "I'm hanging in there."

His energy matches what he says, and it feels as if he is always *coping* with life. In other words, life is happening *to* him. Of course, we all have to cope with what comes up in life, but if we're just "hanging in there" or enduring, we have some major work to do. If your life is less than satisfying, what are you going to do about it? We have the power to create our lives, like Dorothy clicking her heels together, if we just take the reins.

We have a family member who hates his life. He hates his career, a very successful career I might add. He hates his long-term relationship. He will retire soon and move to a different area, but he will still have the same unsatisfying relationship. He's resigned himself to a life of dissatisfaction. Why would you do that to yourself? Is that what he thinks he deserves? Is there some misguided sense of responsibility? I'm not saying to jump ship when a relationship is not life-giving. But I am saying if something isn't working, either fix it or move on. There is always a way out of the box or dilemma. If you haven't thought of it yet, don't despair. If you apply yourself with an open mind and you tell yourself you deserve to be happy, *you will find it*. Remember, we create our own meaning.

Anne was a young woman who desperately wanted to be a mother. She had two miscarriages, and for health reasons, her physician advised against trying again. She was severely depressed. She couldn't imagine how she could find meaning when the thing she wanted the most was not possible. There are always options if someone is *willing* to look. After a while, she was willing to look, and we discussed adoption, fostering, IVF, and surrogacy. When she stopped mourning what she couldn't have, she was able to redirect her energy into what her options were. She and her husband made a different choice for themselves, and they happily found meaning in their new choice.

Our ninety-five-year-old neighbor Ed lived alone, ate crappy food, and smoked Camel non-filtered cigarettes. He found meaning in gardening and especially in tending to his roses. He read a lot. He was in the AA program and was thirty-eight years sober. He kept an active social life by sponsoring people and attending meetings. And he chased the young ladies in their mid-seventies. He was always upbeat and cheerful. It was clear he enjoyed his life, and I believe it was because he created a life that had meaning for *him.* His kids wanted him to do this or that, friends gave him their advice about what he should be doing, but old Eddie just stayed his course and was exceedingly happy because he was living his life *his* way. To do this, you must know who you are and have the courage to blow off criticisms or objections and stay the course.

Where do you find meaning in your life today? When are you the happiest?

Look into the future. What do you think would provide meaning for you there?

Don't stop at one idea, let your imagination run wild!

Chapter 12

Imagination

Imagination is the goose that continuously lays the golden eggs. Believe it! Imagination is one of the most powerful, magical tools at our disposal, and all we have to do is invite it in and give it some floor time. Not only that, what could be more enjoyable than indulging your imagination? *Everything* happens from our "imaging" first. First, we have an idea, then we invest our energy into it, then it materializes. Even if someone else gives us an idea (hey, I saw a job you might like), it doesn't come to life until we invest our energy into it. All the discoveries from the beginning of civilization have sprung from someone's imagination. You don't have to make a world-changing discovery to derive the benefits of a healthy imagination. Excitement, joy, and satisfaction are the results of using our imagination to create something that is new and needed in our lives.

Because of our busy lives, we don't always take the time to dream or languish, just letting thoughts come as they may. Doing that is a worthy endeavor and will produce striking results, if given enough time. If I'm working with someone who wants a better job, a relationship, or a different situation in any arena, I always ask them to imagine what that would look like for them. What specific qualities would this job have?

Here are some things I want out of my career: I want to work for myself, I want to structure my own time, I want to make X amount of money, I want clients that are excited about developing their full potential, I want to be interested and to be challenged, I want to have variety, and I want to help people transform their lives into awesome lives where they're living *their* dream. Another person would have a different list of items that would be important to them, but the key is to clearly imagine what *you* want. Regarding relationships, I have clients imagine what qualities and characteristics they want in a partner. With difficult situations, I ask clients what options they can imagine, even if they seem crazy. In the corporate world, this is called brainstorming, throwing the pasta against the wall to see what sticks.

Sometimes in this world we find ourselves in difficult situations, and we feel as if we're stuck and don't have any options. We may not realize it, but we *always* have options, even if it's just the option of changing our perception of something. To explore options with your imagination is to travel the yellow brick road with hope and magic. Nice to get back to some magic because when our constant thinking and tasking crowds the magic out, life can get a little bit dry.

When I was a child, my family was camping at Lake Wenatchee in Washington. After dinner, Dad and I sat by the campfire talking. It was dark outside and crystal clear, and stars splashed across the sky. I remember my dad saying as he looked up at the sky, "Maybe that's just a piece of cardboard painted black with a light behind it and tiny little pin holes for the light to shine through."

He was being funny, but it was interesting to me, a point of departure, of imagination. For a moment, as I looked at the sky, I pictured it as just that, a light shining through little pin holes behind a piece of cardboard painted black. It was whimsical, crazy, and exciting at the same time. Though I *knew* it wasn't so, it was wild to imagine. My imagination was stretched. I was playing with perceptions.

Another time, when I was just eight, I was visiting Nanna who lived on Vancouver Island. We were alone on that afternoon, and out of the blue, she said to me, "I think there must be life on other planets. What do you think, Gay?"

I was too young to have developed an opinion on this. I had never even heard this topic discussed. Therefore, I was open to pondering rather than having prejudices, which would have immediately closed the door on my imagination. Common sense told me that if there's one planet in the universe that could produce life, there could be others. That went against the common belief at that time, and I thank Nanna for getting to me before the commonly-held beliefs could crowd out my imagination. Nanna's question encouraged my imagination to flourish unabated.

Sometimes our firm beliefs and opinions about things preclude discovery. There's a wonderful Buddhist saying, "He who knows everything learns nothing."

If we set our opinions aside and let our imagination go wild, we come up with ideas and solutions we never thought possible. If I have a client that shoots down all the options I might throw out, I know they actually want to stay stuck. Then *that* is the therapeutic issue that has to be explored. Are there secondary gains for staying stuck? Do I get to play the victim role by being in a seemingly-hopeless situation?

Often I'll ask clients, "If you could have anything you want, what would be your preferred future?"

Sometimes the answer is truly out of reach, but most of the time our preferred future can be constructed with determination, perseverance, and discipline. Even if it's out of reach, the very exercise of imagining enables us to get one step closer to discovering the future things that might engender the feeling we're after. Allow yourself the luxury of fantasizing and see where it takes you. Be especially careful to not interject all your objections. "Oh, I could never do that, have that."

"I'm too old."

"It's too late."

"I don't have the talent."

"That would never happen to me."

"It's unrealistic."

These are simply rationalizations from the subconscious mind that doesn't want change. Change threatens the subconscious mind. it doesn't know you can survive it because you haven't experienced it yet. This is where self-sabotage comes in. Watch for it and head it off at the pass! Realize that it's your birthright that you can grow into something more, and you will not only survive it, but will also thrive in it.

Imagination is what has enabled many of my clients to create new, exciting careers, establish new, satisfying relationships, or the rejuvenation of old ones, and find new solutions for difficult situations or circumstances.

Allow your imagination to have some floor time. You might be surprised and delighted by what comes up.

Take a half hour to an hour a few times a week. Lie down and close your eyes and just let your imagination flow.

Pick a problem that you have and let your imagination go to work on solutions. Think of as many solutions as you can, even if they seem crazy.

You can frame your imagination if you like by asking a question and then sitting back and seeing what comes up. Example: What do I need to change in my life right now?

Chapter 13

New Things

"This is really sexy," Dean whispered in my ear.

If Dean had resisted learning the tango, he never would have experienced how sexy it is. If I had resisted learning to shoot a gun, I would never have felt how empowering it is. I wouldn't have known how good it feels to know I can protect myself and to know I could survive if, for some reason, food was scarce. Neither of us imagined we would develop confidence and esteem by dancing or shooting, but that's the way it works. Anything we master, even on a small scale, builds our esteem.

When we get older, we know a lot of things by heart, and that's great because it's time efficient. We don't have to think things through all the time. But that also has a downside. Life can become stale without new things and new projects. When Dean and I decided to move to the desert to start our internships, Dean's long-time salt-of-the-earth friend looked at us and shook his head and said, "Hair-brained scheme no. 10."

We had to laugh because it was true. We were winging it and hoping for the best. But the point is we wanted something new, some uncharted territory that we would have to master somehow.

I have a friend whose parents lived in a suburb of Seattle until the kids were launched. Then they moved to a condo on Queen Anne Hill; 1,600 square feet, with a deck replacing their huge yard, it was easy to take care of and freed up their time considerably. Seattle was minutes down the hill, where they could easily partake in all the city's activities. They loved it. They were rejuvenated. It was like starting out when they were first married with all kinds of possibilities.

I currently have some young clients who are launching a new business on a shoestring, and California prices, in just about everything, were killing them. They grew up in the desert of Coachella Valley but wanted something new. They moved to a different state that had four seasons and lots of lakes, and they could get twice as much for their money. They can't believe how happy they are. They *love* their new life. All it took was the courage to go for it.

A couple of years ago, Tito, a seventy-nine-year-old client, came in bursting with energy. That always gets my attention. Energy is the name of the game. We asked him what he was doing, and he told us he was on the ketogenic diet and that we should do it. He lost 35 lbs. and the fat around his middle. Now neither Dean nor I need to lose weight, but Tito's energy level enticed us to do some research. What we found would fill a book in itself, but to make a long story short, we decided to give it a whirl. It was tough to adjust to 70 percent fat, 25 percent protein, and 5 percent carbs. That meant no pasta among other things. Remember, Dean's Italian and a great cook.

In two weeks, Dean's knees, which had been killing him for several years, stopped hurting. That stubborn fat on my sides and on Dean's middle (no matter how much we worked out) started gradually melting away. Dean started sleeping better, and we began to notice that our energy levels were increasing. Though it was hard to put into practice, if we weren't willing to try something new, we would never have reaped the benefits. Now though we blow it sometimes, we quickly get back to being in ketosis because we love the way it makes us feel.

Trying something new doesn't mean it always turns out. Sometimes it's an abysmal failure, but so what? It's an experience, and you learn from it and move on. Once we invested in the Swiss franc, touted as the most secure investment in the world. Ours was a ninety-day CD, and within the first thirty days, for the first time in history, the Swiss decided to devalue their currency. You win some, and you lose some in life, but nothing happens standing on the sidelines.

Dean and I have talked about writing a book for years because we both love to write. Late last year, we each finally launched into our individual book projects. Will we get published? Who knows? Are we having a great experience with the artistry of writing a book? Absolutely. Are we growing and learning from the process? No doubt about it. It's a win-win, no matter how it turns out. And in the process, we've enjoyed brainstorming, talking about, and editing each other's books. It's *the process* that has value.

My client Isabel is nearing seventy. She has a career but wanted something new. She decided she wanted to learn how to be a mediator. She went for it, learned it, was successful, and now is pursuing city government. She could have said she was too old, it's too late, she couldn't learn it, no one would hire her. But the truth is she's good at it and people want her. Isabel was willing to learn something new, and it blossomed. Great feelings of esteem were the result.

I had a couple looking for new things to do as a couple as they had grown apart in many ways. They wanted to reconnect and deepen their intimacy. We explored different things that they could do together to get that connection, and one of the things they decided on was ballroom dancing. They got good at it and even won some awards. Not only did it deepen their relationship, but it also gave each of them individually a new sense of confidence. It provided hours of enjoyment, and they made many friends in their new community.

Stephen, a man in his forties who always felt like a klutz, made the decision to learn tennis. It was slow-going, and he was incredibly shy about it, but eventually, learning something new turned his life around. It energized him in an area he did not think possible. This gave Stephen the confidence to try other new things that he had previously thought unattainable. All of a sudden, his life was expanding, and so was his enjoyment of life.

Don't live a life filled with regret. My mother-in-law Yolanda lamented that she never wrote a book or created a painting. After my dad's second wife passed away, he regretted that he had not paid more attention and learned how to cook from her. Carpe diem! Seize the day!

What have you always wanted to do that you've put on the back burner? Think of three new things you could learn that would energize your life.

Challenge yourself. If not now, when?

Chapter 14

Acceptance

No matter how brilliantly we lay out our plans, some things are just outside our control. "The best laid plans of mice and men . . ." Earthquakes, floods, tornadoes, the loss of a loved one, a serious health issue, an economic downturn, being human on this planet is to live in an uncertain world. We strive for certainty, but it's really a lost cause. We can do only what we can do. Better to accept that life is uncertain and work within those parameters. To not be torn asunder, we can learn to accept with grace and dignity whatever life offers up to us and make the most of it. If we develop a sense of security within ourselves, rather than in external circumstances, then we are not blown around like a leaf in the wind.

Back to Abraham Maslow. Maslow discovered that self-actualized individuals had many qualities in common. One of my favorites is *they believe everything happens for a reason, and it serves them.* That means everything, good or bad. Ellen was a graduate student in psychology attending UCLA, and I shared this with her. Exceedingly negative, she snapped, "I don't know if I believe that!"

I said, "Well, if you did believe it, how do you think that would affect you?"

Ellen replied, "I would probably find the jewel in every situation."

We both laughed, and I said, "Maybe you should pretend you believe it."

If you look at life in this way, even the most painful experiences will have value. But sometimes you have to search. My client Mia has a serious health issue. It's not going to get any better. In fact, it will get progressively worse. Working with Mia is a delight as she is always willing to search for the learning in every situation. That might be why her doctor is constantly amazed at how well she's doing compared to others with the same disease. She makes the most of her good days, and when the effects of her drug regimen take her down for days at a time, she does what she can.

That might mean she's in her nightgown for five days. By the way, she now has a repertoire of incredibly beautiful nightgowns. Because she doesn't have the same energy she used to, and it takes more concentrated focus to keep her spirits buoyed, she's not willing to spend time with negative people. This has taught her boundaries. In the old days, friends might call and run down the list of everything that was going wrong in their lives. My client might be on the phone for hours. That's over now.

She realizes her time is valuable, and so is her mental state, and she responds accordingly.

I read about a woman who went through the economic crash of '08 and lost her job. She was a single mother with two kids. Her husband was long gone, and no child support was forthcoming. She and the kids were desperate. When we accept the reality of something, now we can get to work looking for solutions. When we resist reality and whine about it, we just sap our own energy. This family started a business picking up dog shit. It started with their neighbors at first, then they began to get calls. They began to realize that, even in a recession, people would pay a small fee for having their yards cleaned of dog shit every day. Eventually, the business they created supported them.

Mary was a woman I worked with who spent forty years trying to get her mother's approval. My biggest job was to get Mary to accept the reality that her mother would never, ever, give her her approval. She happened to be prettier than her mother and had a more successful marriage and career. Though her mother never came right out and said it, it was obvious that she resented her daughter because she had a better life. Confronting the mother with this would go nowhere as this particular mother was not one who would admit to her feelings. In cases like this, acceptance means to stop trying. Once my client finally realized that her mother was not going to change, then she was free to put her energy elsewhere. Does that mean she stopped loving her mother? Of course not. It just meant she didn't expect different behavior from her mother, so she wasn't constantly disappointed. It also meant she did not continue to invest energy into something that was not fruitful.

This is similar to the parent who tries and tries to get their adult child off drugs or alcohol. Since the impetus to quit using resides in the individual who has the problem, the parent can only provide methods and money. If that's been done once or twice and the child's still using, it's time to accept that they'll quit if they want to, and they won't if they don't. And throwing money after it will not make a bit of difference. In fact, it might prolong the agony.

I work with many people who resist getting old. This is a big one since our culture worships youth. They find themselves miserable with every change in the way their body looks, any health changes, any changes to their perceived prestige in life. Aging happens to all of us, whether we like it or not, and we aren't going to escape it. But if we can accept aging gracefully, without resistance, it will offer up some pearls.

Imagine some of the benefits of aging: You don't care what other people think. Hopefully, you have a decent amount of money. (And if you don't, you can change that.) You know your weaknesses and your strengths, and you play to your strengths. You've made a bunch of mistakes so you know where not to step. There's not much you want anymore, so you're not spending money stupidly and needlessly. Your time becomes more valuable, so you don't waste it with ignorant people, drunk people, or narcissists. You don't fight with others anymore because you know that's a complete waste of time, and it puts a dent in your energy. As far as status goes, you realize you probably never had it to begin with. You just created that story in your own mind. If people fawned over you before (like the CEO of a company or a sports or Hollywood star), the truth is they didn't even know you. They just bought the story.

And your looks? The most beautiful people in the world are those who are happy and secure within themselves, at any age. Their joy is externalized in their appearance. The spirit of a person shines through, no matter what age they are. It impacts how a person looks. I've seen old people with lined faces that are absolutely stunning because the beauty inside them is radiating out. And I've seen young people with flawless faces that look mean or arrogant and are, therefore, unattractive. You can be beautiful at any age, if you take care of yourself, if you are loving and kind, if you are joyous in your life. Don't resist the inevitable. Accept it with dignity and grace.

What are you currently resisting accepting?

If you accepted this/these thing/s, would there be a difference in how you feel? What steps might you take as a result of your acceptance?

Chapter 15

Boundaries

Boundaries are probably the biggest therapeutic issue. Most of us come from families with lousy boundaries, so we're programmed to follow suit. The problem is, with lousy boundaries, *all* relationships suffer, it doesn't matter whether it's your best friend, your boss at work, your kids, a family member, or your lover. Boundaries are crucial in any healthy relationship, and you're never too old to learn how to have them. To establish boundaries, you have to know who you are. Boundaries free us from resentment because the truth is it's us and only us who are responsible for our own experiences.

Learning to have boundaries catapults our growth, and I do mean *catapults*. Why is developing boundaries such a fast track in terms of growth? Think of this: First, we have to go deep inside and examine ourselves and be honest about who we are and what we want (honest self-evaluation). Second, we have to have the courage to put whatever it is out there. And third, we have to stand behind it. Boundaries aren't about hurting anyone else or doing anything to anyone else. They are simply about having the courage to be clear about who we are and the courage to keep ourselves safe.

When I was in my early twenties, I had a good friend who was very depressed. We'd get together once a week and go to dinner and a movie, and I listened as she woefully recounted all the supposedly insurmountable problems in her life. I shared thoughts and made suggestions, which she quickly rejected, and at the end of the evening, I went home thoroughly exhausted. Though I never said so, inside, I was furious, but I thought I was being a good friend. Looking deeply, I realized that underneath the anger were feelings of frustration and helplessness. I could do nothing to change my friend's state. In fact, every suggestion I made was shut down. I was doing all the work, which is why I felt exhausted and angry, while she just sat back feeling sorry for herself and soaking up the attention and sympathy. She was the only one with the power to change herself.

At that same time, I joined a therapy group, and the other participants were older and more experienced. I started learning about boundaries. After some time, I had a serious talk with my friend. I told her I no longer wanted to get together when she was depressed. In fact, if she was depressed, I told her she could call at the very last minute and cancel, and I would not be upset. In addition, I told her that if she wanted to tell me how horrible her life was, I would listen to her once a month, wholeheartedly, for ten minutes. Her response surprised me. She cried and said, "You're the last one."

She had burned off all her friends but me, and I realized I had been enabling her for almost two years. She wasn't about to lose her last friend, so she turned on a dime.

I put down a clear boundary with my friend. But what if she hadn't turned on a dime? It would have been a win-win for me either way. Either she changed and we could once more enjoy each other's company or the bummer evenings were over for me. Now I want to make a distinction. If I had a friend who was situationally depressed, I would be right there to support them. But this friend was chronically depressed and made no effort to climb out of it until I laid down a boundary.

The interesting thing about this story is I found myself mad at my friend because she was draining my batteries. I was blaming her, but I was the real problem: I had lousy boundaries. I came to realize that I, and I alone, am in charge of my own experiences, and boundaries are necessary for me to get the experiences I want. Delivering this boundary with my friend was not easy. In fact, I had anxiety about doing it, partially because I was not used to delivering boundaries but also because I had guilt. When I examined my guilt, I uncovered a faulty belief. I thought a good friend was always supportive, and I always wanted to be a good friend. But enabling isn't being a good friend, a good parent, a good spouse, a good anything. When you enable, you block another's growth. Once you realize this, you can let go of the guilt.

New realizations will come as a result of putting down boundaries. To create a boundary, you must get in touch with how you feel. That allows you to take a look at your faulty beliefs and work through them as I did in the above story. Boundaries have the added benefit of finding out who you're really dealing with by flushing out someone's true intentions. Do they really care about how you feel? If they don't, do you want a friend, partner, or boss who doesn't care about your feelings?

My friend Sally was chronically late by twenty to thirty minutes whenever we had a luncheon engagement. I didn't take it personally as we ran in the same circles, and I knew she was late with everyone, but it still left me angry. The next time it happened, I said, "I'd like to share some feelings with you."

I let Sally know that when she was late, I felt unimportant and not considered since I always made sure I was on time. Sally responded to me by changing her behavior. Clearly, she cared how I felt. If she hadn't responded favorably, once again, I would have lost nothing. It would have shown me she didn't care about my feelings, and who wants a friend who doesn't care about your feelings? This is how you flush someone out.

It doesn't always go the way you like as in this example, but it always goes in your best interest.

Christine had a boyfriend who was wonderful 95 percent of the time, but every nine months or so, he would turn into a raging maniac toward her. These episodes were highly dramatic and completely unreasonable, and they left her feeling as if she'd been run over by a truck. She tried every approach to reach him when he behaved like this, but he was like a moving target—nothing worked. You can have the most delicious soup in front of you, but if there's a fly in it, it spoils everything. After another miserable trip caused by his raging, she spent the weekend thinking.

Christine had to look deep inside herself and be honest about what kind of life she wanted, then she had to have the courage to support herself in getting that life. Since most often these incidents happened when he was drinking, she put down a boundary. She told him, she had gotten clear, she did not want to be with someone who drank. She didn't reprimand him, tell him what a jerk he was, or tell him what to do. Christine just told him what she was going to do. It could have gone either way, but either way it was a win, and she understood that.

We have to be willing to lose when we put down a boundary. If you don't mean it, don't say it. Then it's just manipulation, and it has no power. We don't really lose, but it might feel like that at the moment. In the above example, Christine probably would have felt as if she was losing her boyfriend if he blew her off, but at the same time, she was consciously choosing to have the peaceful life that she wanted. That's a win. And if he blew her off? Good to know now rather than later that this individual would rather continue on with destructive behavior rather than take steps to correct it.

Ron's siblings and parents would drop by the house at any time unannounced. Neither Ron nor his wife wanted these visits. Underneath, they felt anger and irritation, but they didn't want to appear impolite. They loved their family, but that didn't mean they wanted surprise visits. They sacrificed themselves to not hurt their family members. The problem was then they resented their family members. They finally got the courage up to tell their family that they would like them to call before they came over. That way, if it was an inconvenient time, they could let them know. Clarity is good for everyone. You know where you stand and can adjust accordingly.

Boundaries set you free. Often, as soon as a decision has been made to put down a boundary, an individual finds himself taking a sigh of relief. Things are clear, no more ongoing machinations of the mind. In the above example, this couple no longer had to continuously feel anger and frustration with their family members because they had the courage to take care of the problem by setting a boundary.

Kathleen was a woman whose husband was diagnosed with type 2 diabetes. He ate junk, drank and smoked, was at least 75 lbs. overweight, and got no exercise at all. She nagged, pleaded, cajoled, cried, begged to get him to change his behavior, all to no avail. In time, I got her to see that she was not responsible for his choices. She was, however, responsible for hers. The writing was on the wall for this gentleman. He did nothing to take care of himself to offset the disease. Even his doctor told him he was traveling a treacherous path with his behavior.

Kathleen felt guilty about putting down a boundary, you know, the whole "for better or worse" line in the marriage vows. But what about her? Did he think of her? Did he stop and think that he was forcing her into a contract that she had no part in creating or agreeing to? Was it fair for this man to continue a behavior that would ensure his wife becomes a caregiver in a cycle of illness, horrendous surgeries, and medical costs, *and* become the sole support of the family? It would be different if the husband had a disease that could not be helped by any means. Then "for better or worse" would apply. Eventually, Kathleen put down a boundary for her husband: "I will not stand by and watch while you slowly kill yourself. If you are willing to work toward your health, I will be right there by your side."

Sadly, this was not the case, but Kathleen was able to move on with a clear conscience as her husband continued to careen toward self-destruction.

Todd came to see me regarding his wife who had a drinking problem. She had several DUIs and had been in a couple of accidents. He was worried she might kill someone, maybe even their two young children. We discussed the serious consequences of her behavior that would affect him and his children dramatically. He was aware of them, worried about them incessantly, but felt helpless to do anything about it. He lived in a constant state of hypervigilance, like somehow, magically, he could control his wife's drinking. Historically, he knew that wasn't true. His wife was the only one who could do that.

Finally, he learned to put down a boundary. As soon as he made the decision, he was relieved. He found his way out of his dilemma. He let his wife know she either quit drinking completely, immediately, or he would file for a divorce—her choice. If they divorced, he informed her he would go through the courts to insist on alcohol testing and supervised visitation with the kids as he could not trust her to be sober. With her record of two DUIs and an accident, the courts would readily agree. When she realized he was solid in his conviction, she turned her life around. She wasn't about to lose her children and her marriage. This was a win for everyone, especially the kids.

Where are your boundaries weak? How does that make you feel?

Scan your life and choose three areas where it would be profitable for you to set down a firm boundary.

Notice what faulty beliefs come up when you imagine yourself implementing each boundary.

Work through those faulty beliefs.

Then implement your boundaries, one by one. Don't overwhelm yourself by taking on too many at a time. It pays to feel the difference as each boundary is implemented. This will motivate you to set healthy boundaries in the future.

Chapter 16

Mindset

What a difference a mindset makes! It doesn't take long to get a take on someone's mindset. You will identify a person with a growth mindset by the individual's exuberance and zest for life. A growth mindset is defined as a belief that intelligence and abilities are malleable and can be improved. A person with a growth mindset is always learning.

A fixed mindset is the belief that intelligence and abilities cannot be developed. If you believe this, you can see why you would just accept the status quo in every arena.

Here are some examples:

That's just the way I am.

He/she will never change.

We're never going to get anywhere in this relationship.

I'm not athletic.

I'm not artistic.

That's just what we do in this family.

I'll always have a temper.

I could never do that.

I could never say that.

It will never change. That's just the way it is.

I'll never be able to communicate in that way. I don't have the aptitude for that.

Goals like that are too lofty for someone like me. I can't do it.

The fixed mindset is easily identified when someone drags a resistant partner into therapy. People with a growth mindset love therapy, but people with a fixed mindset fear it. In truth, their fears are not unfounded. Change is on the way, and for individuals who hate change, it's an uncomfortable prospect. Some people unconsciously sabotage their partner when they begin individual therapy. They worry that their partner will outgrow them. That's absolutely a possibility, unless they are growing too. People intuitively feel that therapy is going to change things, and to a fixed mindset, that's a threat.

When we've developed a way of being with someone, an energy dynamic, I like to call it, people don't like it when we change the dance steps. It's a challenge for all of us of course, but in particular, it challenges one with a fixed mindset. After Dean and I learned how to communicate appropriately, he had a chance to play it out with a sibling.

We were in the car, heading to Borrego Springs, one day when a sibling called with a head of stream about something. Rather than joining his sibling in a heat, which was the usual dynamic between the two, Dean remained calm and poised. Instead of engaging in a heated conversation and sending criticisms and barbs back and forth, Dean simply expressed his truth and his feelings without resorting to criticism or blaming. His sibling became madder and madder.

Dean changed the dance steps, and it was clear his sibling felt more and more out of control. Why did his sibling become so upset? Because it wasn't the usual dance that had been their lifelong pattern. If his sibling wanted to communicate with him in the future, new dance steps would need to be learned.

Sometimes we can have a rigid mindset in one area and a growth mindset in another. I don't believe we're stuck with a particular mindset. We often learn mindsets from our parents or our environment when we're young. Educating clients about mindset has stimulated incredible growth in them. When clients become aware of a fixed mindset in themselves, they are then able to evaluate if it serves them. More often than not, they see that shifting their mindset from fixed to growth opens up new vistas of opportunity.

Let me give you a personal example. When we bought our house in Sedona, we had a lot of fixing up to do. We were spending lots of time and money turning it into a beautiful place. For a small house, I was shocked when the painting estimates for the inside all came in at over $4,000. Dean said, "Let's paint it ourselves and use that money elsewhere on the house."

I responded, "I'm a terrible painter, I hate to paint."

In painting experiences, I always started out well, and then I would get impatient, get sloppy, and end up covered with paint. But I thought about it. Why cling to my fixed mindset that I'm a terrible painter? Maybe I could be an excellent painter.

So I decided I would become an excellent painter. Lo and behold, I became an excellent painter. I knew my weakness was impatience, so I decided I would take my time, as long as it took, to do it well in an impeccable way. We opted to play relaxing spa music while we painted to learn to *enjoy the process* rather than rushing to get the result. I now realize that though painting isn't my favorite thing, I am an excellent painter. If we can change our mindset in one area to get better results, we can do it in another.

Identify your mindset in different areas of your life.

Where you have a fixed mindset, contemplate whether it would be advantageous to shift it.

How might that feel? Remember, everything you master builds self-esteem.

Chapter 17

Presence

What does presence really mean? When we say someone has a "presence," I think we're saying that this individual is bringing "more" to the table. They're more conscious. We see it in a great spiritual soul, a true political leader, an incredible actor, or the guy next door who's just totally conscious. Presence means "being here now." It's focusing totally on what we're doing right now. It's being present for what is unfolding in front of us.

Ever tried to have a conversation with someone while they continue to check their phone, eye what's on their desk, or flip through their mail?

Many people pride themselves on being multitaskers, and I understand. Our culture holds that up as some sort of accomplishment. But is it really? Are we missing something? New data suggest that we don't do things as well when we're doing many things at once. The Navy SEALs say it doesn't matter how smart you are, if you're thinking of five things at once, you'll have a brain freeze. Juggling five balls in the air may be an exciting challenge, but we might miss the cat flying through the air chasing a butterfly.

The Buddhists say, "When you eat, eat. When you walk, walk. When you sit, sit." In other words, *be with* whatever you're doing. When you're eating, don't diffuse your energy by going through the mail, watering the plants, putting in a load of laundry, or checking your phone for messages. Try to be present with one activity and *experience it fully*. This is easier said than done (I can tell you!) but well worth the effort. *It is restorative.* Most of us are not good at this, but we can learn, especially if we understand the benefits we get by doing it. This is akin to going deep rather than wide.

Imagine this: We all have a battery within us containing a certain amount of energy. Suppressing old hurts and feelings depletes that energy. It requires ongoing energy to keep those uncomfortable feelings buried. Now we have less voltage to access. Now perhaps we're also procrastinating on a project that needs to get done—another drain on our voltage. Or maybe we're engaging in an on-going battle with our sister-in-law—another drain on our battery. Now out of a 12-volt battery, maybe we can access 4 volts. Does that give us the required energy to create the lives we want? I don't think so. One of the goals of therapy is to bring those feelings out, work through them, and let them go. Then our voltage isn't sucked up by nonsense. We can access 100 percent of our energy to put toward whatever we choose. When we can access all our energy, it comes across as *presence*.

Today I was having lunch with my wonderful friend, Linda. I met Linda after I had searched for eight long years to find a great hypnotherapist to join us at the office. In our encounters, we always discuss what's going on in life and things we're working on. *She is a fellow traveler.* Today I noticed we had each dropped a major individual goal. Does that mean we're giving the goal up? Not at all. It just means we want all our energy going to the projects we currently have without getting overwhelmed and diluting our energy with too much going on.

We will get back to that goal at a future date if it's still relevant, perhaps when some current goals have been completed. To be present, you have to sometimes create the space for presence. You want your life to be fun and joyous, not stressful. Making sure we're living in the now, not in the past or in the future, helps us get there. The fastest way to be present is to *pay attention.*

How present do you think you are in your life?

Notice the times when you are really not present. If you imagine being present in those times, how do you think that would change your enjoyment of life?

What are some actions you could take that would allow you to be more present?

Chapter 18

Creativity

Imagine sailing through the water, surfing the perfect wave. That's the feeling of creativity in action. We can all think of times when our creativity flowed, and what did we feel? A euphoria that was vital and energizing. It could be anything: putting together the perfect deal, painting a watercolor, designing anything, building anything, *creating the life you want*. Creativity is the "bringing forth" of what's bubbling inside us.

If you want to get in touch with your creativity, you want to engage your muses. Muses are finicky. They have to be courted. They don't just show up for anybody. They have to know you really mean it. You have to invite them in, and then space and time must be created for them to do their magic. Once befriended, your muses will lay out the red carpet for you. They are the gift that keeps on giving. But you have to be consistent to hold their attention and be worthy of their help.

In her book, *The Creative Habit*, Twayla Tharp, the aforementioned choreographer, describes what it takes to be creative: *habit. Your established habit* provides your muses with what they need. You've often heard stories of artists who set up a prescribed time every day whether they have any ideas flowing or not. They know that ideas will come forth if they make room for them.

If I have a client who comes in with a particular problem, I'll sometimes ask them, "What would be a creative solution to that?"

More often than not, *I* get energized by the amazing ideas they come up with. The ideas were in there. The clients were just so focused on the problem that their creativity was eclipsed. People are often surprised by their own creative ideas. I believe that's because we don't cultivate the creative habit.

Creative solutions are often the most difficult to come up with in emotional and relational dynamics. Sometimes an individual is very creative in business, but when it comes to solving emotional issues with their creativity, they don't even think of it. The emotions cloud the creative solutions.

Nancy had a situation with her elderly mother, who had some health problems and could no longer drive. Nancy knew that if her mother came to live with her, her life would be hell. Though she loved her mother dearly, whenever they spent too much time together, they both got irritable. But her mother refused to go into assisted care. Nancy felt stuck, like there was no way out. She almost succumbed to allowing her mother to live with her and choosing to become a permanent victim.

Creative options are almost always there. You just have to diligently search. In this case, the creative solution was to buy a duplex. Nancy could give her mother the safety of knowing she was right next door if anything should happen. She brought in a caregiver for a few hours every day. Nancy took her mother shopping a couple of times a week, and they sometimes had dinner together. This way, they maintained the enjoyment of the relationship, with each having their own life.

I have some clients who have a huge house with beautiful grounds. They got tired of caring for it and wanted to travel more. They decided to see if there was a market for renting it out. Since the Coachella Valley is home to big events, such as Stagecoach, Coachella Fest, and the Indian Wells Masters Tennis Tournament, they discovered the house would be in demand. It's ideal for weddings and big venues. This set my clients free. Instead of selling their house, they not only created freedom, but also a hefty income for themselves.

Covid-19 forced everyone to create new ways of operating: new, creative ways of doing business, communicating with others, going to school, even traveling (try to buy an Airstream these days). Necessity is the mother of invention—no joke. How about the invention of cryptocurrency? And now the creation of DeFi (decentralized finance)? Or wow, the private sector going into space. The sky's not the limit in terms of our creativity if we engage it. If you haven't watched the movie *The Boy Who Harnessed the Wind*, now's the time. Inspire yourself!

Being in the flow of creativity is naturally a very exciting place to be. Even little spurts of creativity can generate excitement. I remember one Easter when Dean's brother and girlfriend came for a visit. Even though we are all adults, I got the idea to put together a treasure hunt. Dean and I had as much fun choosing the clues and hiding places as his brother and girlfriend had in finding them. The process of creating is the fun part. The end, the goal, is icing on the cake.

Many years ago a friend and I wanted to buy a house in Santa Barbara. We didn't have a down payment, but we were determined to find a way. We started looking at all the ways to creatively finance and, after wading through a lot of dross, came upon a couple who was willing to do shared equity. They put down the down payment. We handled the mortgage payment, ongoing costs, and all the remodeling. The result, a beautiful little house on Bath Street in Santa Barbara. At the end of our contract, we could either buy out the investors or sell the property and split the proceeds. Everybody told us there was no way we could get a house without having a substantial down payment. *When you hear "No, it can't be done, there's no way out of this dilemma," keep on thinking.*

When was the last time you felt your creative juices flowing? What were the circumstances?

Are you aware of how you feel when you're being creative?

For a problem you have now, what would be some creative solutions?

Set aside some time for your creativity to flow. Personify it. Ask your creativity, what do you want me to express? Then journal what comes forth without judgment.

Chapter 19

Having a Voice

Having a voice is supporting yourself. Many people stifle their voice out of fear of abandonment, fear of being judged, fear of a reaction, or fear of being embarrassed. When you don't have a voice, it is the equivalent of abandoning yourself. This is a cardinal sin. If you want a healthy self, you *never, ever,* abandon yourself. It's ironic, isn't it? The fear of being abandoned causes one to abandon oneself. That's the last thing you ever want to do. If you do, you can count on your self-esteem taking a nosedive. All of us can look back on our lives and remember a time when we've abandoned ourselves and, in the wake of that, experienced the wreckage of our self-esteem.

So why is having a voice so important? I like to use a sexual analogy here. Think of this: Everything in nature has a beginning, a middle, and an end. Spring follows winter, summer follows spring, fall follows summer. We're born, we grow old, we die. Everything has a season. Right, back to the sexual analogy. Imagine that you start at square one in a relaxed state. Then you and your partner start fooling around. Your physiology starts to change, and you start getting aroused (the beginning). In time, you have an orgasm (the middle), then your physiology starts to calm down, and soon you're back at the initial relaxed state (the end), *but you're satisfied.* The key word here is *satisfied.* You've completed a natural cycle of beginning, middle, and end and are left with the afterglow of *completion.* But what if after the first phase of arousal, for some reason, you didn't have an orgasm? How did you feel? Most people report that they feel disappointed, angry, depressed, or anxious. That's because the natural cycle has been interrupted or truncated.

The same feelings arise when expression is stifled. Expression, or having a voice, also has a beginning, middle, and end. Thoughts and feelings well up in our heads and hearts (the beginning), and the natural desire is to express them (the middle). If we are able to have a voice and express ourselves, then we bring the cycle to its satisfactory conclusion (the end).

If we fear doing that for whatever reason, we truncate the process and are left with feelings of dismay.

Sometimes, in therapy, a client will say something that's right on, and they shock themselves. Hearing what they say aloud makes them aware of something that they previously obfuscated from their vision. I might ask a client, "What percentage of the time are you miserable in your relationship with your wife/husband?"

"Oh, about 75 percent of the time," they might answer, scarcely believing what just came out of their mouth.

Wow, 75 percent chance of misery, would you take those odds to Vegas? What they voiced out loud really put things into perspective for them.

I encouraged my client Karen who had been physically abused by her father as a child to speak to him about it and share how it had hurt her. She was sure he would just explode, so what's the point? The point is no matter what reaction you get, you've supported yourself by having a voice. The reaction is irrelevant. The work is done by expressing. Of course, it's always nice to be well received, but that doesn't always happen. If it does happen, it's icing on the cake. And hoping for a good reaction is not the proper motivation. You could be sorely disappointed. Karen was not ready to confront her father. She was afraid. The childhood pattern of fearing her father continued to follow her into her adult life. But the seeds were planted. She now understood *why* having a voice would benefit her. By confronting, she could let go of resentment (having said her piece) as well as the fear of her father. (She's an adult now, not a little girl, and she can protect herself.)

Several months later, Karen came into session with a spring in her step. I asked her what was going on, and she told me she had a breakthrough over the weekend. She shared with me that she had confronted her father (gracefully, just sharing feelings, not condemning), and he gave her a sincere apology, knowing his behavior had been harsh. The beauty of this situation and how it turned out is that this freed the father from years of suffering from the guilt of how he had behaved. He was well aware of what he'd done but didn't have the courage to bring it up because it was so painful. Because she conquered her fear and confronted it, she set them both free.

Suzanne had been dating a man for ten years and wondering if they were ever going to have a future together. I asked her why she didn't ask him directly if they were going to have a future together. She said she didn't want to appear like other women, always pushing to get married. But the truth was she *did* want to secure a future with him. She wanted clarity but was afraid to ask for it because she was afraid of how she might appear. Finally, Suzanne was able to step up and ask for clarity. Did they have a future together? The answer was no. She'd wasted ten years of her life hoping but not clarifying. Upon reflection, she realized that she had known intuitively that the answer was no. She didn't ask because she didn't want the answer. Having a voice brings clarity.

Suki was a client who brought a project idea to her husband. He was cranky and irritated and poked holes in her idea, making her feel as if it was not valid or well thought out. It wasn't a good feeling. She went into their study and wrote out a script of how she would have liked the conversation to go. When Suki was finished, she went back out to her husband and said, "Let's start over. I've written a script of how I would like our conversation to go for me to feel loved and supported."

Her husband laughed as he went through it with her, and it lightened the mood entirely. It was not as if she wanted agreement—an idea is an idea. We might like it, we might not. But Suki was able to have a voice and let her husband know that his attitude left her with negative feelings. She was also very specific (the script) about how he could leave her with positive feelings, whether he agreed with her idea or not. This creative approach left them both with good feelings.

Where do you not have a voice? How does that make you feel?

What is the fear that stops you from having a voice?

See if you can imagine having a voice in that area and what that would feel like.

Find another area where you do not have a voice and go through the above exercise.

Chapter 20

Spirituality

Belief in God is a wild and wooly topic these days, inviting speculation and a massive amount of controversy. But why is everyone getting so hot and bothered? Isn't this a personal matter?

When I think of our bodies and our minds and how everything works together to produce a living human being, I am amazed. When I think of all the systems of the earth and sky working in unison to produce the colorful life on this planet, I'm filled with awe. Complex, intricate systems feeding into one another, forming the perfect design, to me, this is *divine intelligence or God.*

We can call the origin of this amazing universe divine intelligence, God, Christ, Krishna, Buddha, The Tao, or the great spirit. The label is not important, but knowing that there is something greater than ourselves in operation gets us in touch with the mystery of life. Connecting with that divine source is a thrill, working with it, making it operational in our lives. Having a connection with the spirit transforms a "dry" life into a "juicy" life. It's like having your own spiritual guide (or the Good Witch) riding right alongside you.

I have noticed it has become increasingly vogue to be atheist these days. It's another one of those "social contagions." People announce proudly that they're atheists, like they're on the cutting edge of something, the zeitgeist of the new millennium, or the intelligencia. But atheism has been around forever. There's nothing new or different about it. There's nothing wrong with being an atheist or an agnostic or a believer. All these are simply belief systems, and people are entitled to their own belief systems. But to know ourselves, it's important to inquire into why we have adopted particular belief systems. If we look carefully, we can see that vogue beliefs attract adherents simply because they're vogue. With that, there's pressure to conform, implicitly and explicitly. People like to be in the "in crowd."

Some choose atheism to feel intellectually superior, yet there are many intellectual icons who believe in God. Just as some choose religion to feel morally superior, and we sometimes find that the behavior just doesn't match with the morals. Either of these motivations preclude the deep thinking that, right or wrong, provides a solid foundation for our beliefs.

Just seeing the reflection of the sky in a raindrop, a rainbow spanning the sky, convinces me that there is a divine source or intelligence. What could be more amazing than that? How about an Olympic runner breaking yet another record, taking a call on our Apple Watch, seeing private companies going into space, watching a new home unfold in an hour from a 8.5-foot box? It would take an eternity to list all the stunning things in the universe. Our feelings of awe, appreciation and gratitude transform a black-and-white life into brilliant color.

Many years ago, I had a spiritual experience that left me with a "knowing" rather than a "belief." It doesn't matter what anybody says to me, *I know*. What do I know? I know there's something larger than myself. I sense that energy is loving and good. I know that when I connect with that energy, my life becomes more exciting. For weeks after this experience, I was on an unbelievable high. Nothing bothered me. I was completely at peace living in a state of perpetual enjoyment.

Gradually, this state of being waned, but I never fell completely back to where I was before. This experience was a gift of grace. It showed me that there was so much more to life than I had imagined. It taught me that there were states of being that were blissful, expansive, and joyous and that we could learn to access them.

Variations of "ask and you shall receive" can be found in countless spiritual texts. But what does that really mean? Most of us don't believe there's an old man in the sky with a long beard who's calling the shots. So what then? If we believe in a divine intelligence, how would we access this? Are we worthy to access it? A dream I had gave me some insight.

I saw a man walking two large cats on a leash. They were the size of bobcats. I thought, *No way, no cat will put up with that.*

But as I watched in fascination, the cats were actually enjoying it, moving in sync with the man. My eyes then fell to five little kittens bouncing along clumsily in the wake of the big cats. Everyone in this scene—man, cats, and kittens—seemed joyous and in a "synchronistic" groove.

With Jungian dream analysis, everyone in the dream is an aspect of your "self." I broke down each item to discover what it represented to me.

The man: The part of myself that wants to take action, create, take my goods to the world (the male energy).

The leash: Connection.

The cats: Spirit. Here, spirit is harnessed by the man, and the cats clearly enjoyed being harnessed by him and moving in sync with him.

The kittens: The five creations (progeny) as a result of the marriage of man and spirit. According to numerology, the number 5 represents *freedom, curiosity, change,* and *new possibilities.*

This is what the dream illustrated to me: Divine intelligence is aching for us to create a portal to allow it to come in and assist us. *It loves to work with us. After all, its nature is to create.* If you don't believe me, check out the universe. *And when man and spirit are united in purpose, creative offspring are the result.* You are a wave that is part of the "big sea." You are not unworthy. Nothing closes the portal faster than that belief.

If you have even an inkling of God or divine intelligence, court it, invite it in, make it real and operational in your life. Realize you are a part of it. See for yourself how connecting with this source gives you perspective and enriches your life.

Think deeply and honestly. What is the origin of your belief system? What are the benefits or the drawbacks of your belief system?

What feelings do you experience as a result of your belief system?

If you do believe in something greater, how could you get in touch with that and make it operational in your life?

Chapter 21

Coming Home

Creating the life you want is actually an art. It isn't hard, but you do have to roll up your sleeves and give it the time and effort to come up with your ideal design. Your goal is clarity. It's as much about clearing away what you don't want as it is about adding what you do.

Without using your brain to design your life, life becomes unrealistic and the stuffing falls out of it just like the Scarecrow. Without integrating your heart, life becomes dry and rigid like the Tinman. You need to incorporate both. Your brain (the Scarecrow) and your heart (the Tin Man) together are an unbeatable team. All you need then is courage (the Lion) to make your dreams come true.

Take the first step to make the rest the best. The time is now. There will never be a better time to start. Begin your journey, open your mind to possibilities, realize you're awesome, and look forward to reaping the amazing rewards of a fully-actualized life. *Experience your greatness.* Experiencing your greatness is not boastful or arrogant. It's simply getting in touch with your true nature, *which is creative.* Expanding our potential is not just available to a select few. It's available to all of us, if we truly apply ourselves. Jim Rohm says it best, "If you really want to do something, you'll find a way. If you don't, you'll find an excuse."

Remember the end of *The Wizard of Oz?* To get home, all Dorothy had to do was click her heels together three times. (In numerology, the number 3 represents magic, intuition, fecundity, and advantage.) The Good Witch let it be known that Dorothy had the ability to go home all along. But Dorothy had to discover this for herself. The trials and tribulations she experienced lead her to uncover what *she always had but didn't realize.* This book is about uncovering your true self, reaching your full potential, and *becoming self-actualized.* The rewards for your efforts? Living a life that's *happy, successful,* and *free.*

"You are never to old to set another goal or to dream another dream"

C.S.Lewis

MAKE THE REST, THE BEST!

You can contact Dr. Gay Matheson to arrange private
consultations or speaking engagements.

Send an email to: gaymatheson11@gmail.com